EUROPEAN
UNIVERSALISM

EUROPEAN UNIVERSALISM

The Rhetoric of Power

IMMANUEL WALLERSTEIN

THE NEW PRESS

NEW YORK
LONDON

Requests for permission to reproduce selections from this book
should be mailed to: Permissions Department, The New Press,
38 Greene Street, New York, NY 10013

Published in the United States by The New Press, New York, 2006
Distributed by W. W. Norton & Company, Inc., New York

LIBRARY OF CONGRESS CATALOGING-IN-PUBLICATION DATA

The New Press was established in 1990 as a not-for-profit
alternative to the large, commercial publishing houses currently
dominating the book publishing industry. The New Press
operates in the public interest rather than for private gain,
and is committed to publishing, in innovative ways, works
of educational, cultural, and community value that are often
deemed insufficiently profitable.

www.thenewpress.com

Book design by XXXXX
Composition by dix!
This book was set in Granjon

Printed in the United States of America

10   9   8   7   6   5   4   3   2   1

To Anouar Abdel-Malek,
who has spent his life trying to foster
a more universal universalism

CONTENTS

PREFACE:
THE POLITICS OF
UNIVERSALISM TODAY

The headlines of the world's newspapers are filled with familiar terms: al-Qaeda, Iraq, Kosovo, Rwanda, the gulag, globalization, and terrorism. They evoke instant images for readers, and these images have been shaped for us by our political leaders and the commentators on the world scene. For many, the world today is a struggle between the forces of good and the forces of evil. And we all wish to be on the side of good. While we may debate the wisdom of particular policies to fight evil, we tend to be in no doubt that we ought to fight evil, and we are often in not much doubt as to who and what incarnates evil.

The rhetoric of the leaders of the pan-European world—in particular, but not only, the United States and Great Britain—and the mainstream media and Establishment intellectuals is filled with appeals to universalism as the basic justification of their policies. This is especially so when they talk about their policies relating to the "others"—the countries of the non-European world, the populations of the poorer and "less developed" nations. The tone is often righteous, hectoring, and arrogant, but the policies are always presented as reflecting universal values and truths.

There are three main varieties of this appeal to universalism. The first is the argument that the policies pursued by the leaders of the pan-European world are in defense of "human rights" and in furtherance of something called "democracy." The second comes in the jargon of the clash of civilizations, in which it is always assumed that "Western" civilization is superior to "other" civilizations because it is the only one that has come to be based on these universal values and truths. And the third is the assertion of the scientific truths of the market, the concept that "there is no alternative" for governments but to accept and act on the laws of neoliberal economics.

Read any speech of George W. Bush or Tony Blair in recent years (and indeed, the speeches of their predecessors), or any of their many acolytes, and you will find the constant reiteration of these three themes. These are not new themes, however. As I shall try to demonstrate in this book, they are instead very old themes, which have constituted the basic rhetoric of the powerful throughout the history of the modern world-system, since at least the sixteenth century. There is a history to this rhetoric. And there is a history of opposition to this rhetoric. In the end, the debate has always revolved around what we mean by universalism. I shall seek to show that the universalism of the powerful has been a partial and distorted universalism, one that I am calling "European universalism" because it has been put forward by pan-European leaders and intellectuals in their quest to pursue the interests of the dominant strata of the modern world-system. Moreover, I shall discuss the ways in which we might instead move forward to a genuine universalism, what I am calling "universal universalism."

The struggle between European universalism and universal universalism is the central ideological struggle of the contemporary world, and its outcome will be a major factor in determining how the future world-system into which we shall be entering in the next twenty-five to fifty years will be structured. We cannot avoid taking sides. And we cannot retreat into some super-particularist stance, in which we invoke the equal validity of every particularist idea put forward across the globe. For super-particularism is nothing but a hidden surrender to the forces of European universalism and the powerful of the present, who are seeking to sustain their inegalitarian and undemocratic world-system. If we are to construct a real alternative to the existing world-system, we must find the path to enunciating and institutionalizing universal universalism—a universalism that is possible to achieve, but that will not automatically or inevitably come into realization.

The concepts of human rights and democracy, the superiority of Western civilization because it is based on universal values and truths, and the inescapability of submission to the "market" are all offered to us as self-evident ideas. But they are not at all self-evident. They are complex ideas that need to be analyzed carefully, and stripped of their noxious and nonessential parameters, in order to be evaluated soberly and put at the service of everyone rather than a few. Understanding how these ideas came to be asserted originally, by whom and to what ends, is a necessary part of this task of evaluation. It is a task to which this book seeks to contribute.

ACKNOWLEDGMENTS

In November 2004, I was invited by St. John's College of the University of British Columbia to be its first Distinguished Lecturer in the Perspective of the World. I was asked to give a series of three lectures. This text is the revised version of those lectures, with a fourth chapter added in which I draw the general conclusions of my argument. I am extremely appreciative of the invitation by the principal of St. John's, Professor Timothy Brook, to speak at the college, and the helpful and responsive reactions by the audience to my lectures.

EUROPEAN
UNIVERSALISM

I

Whose Right to Intervene? Universal Values Against Barbarism

The history of the modern world-system has been in large part a history of the expansion of European states and peoples into the rest of the world. This has been an essential part of the construction of a capitalist world-economy. The expansion has involved, in most regions of the world, military conquest, economic exploitation, and massive injustices. Those who have led and profited most from this expansion have presented it to themselves and the world as justified on the grounds of the greater good that such expansion has had for the world's populations. The usual argument is that the expansion has spread something variously called civilization, economic growth and development, and/or progress. All of these words have been interpreted as expressions of universal values, encrusted in what is often called natural law. Therefore, it has been asserted that this expansion was not merely beneficial to humankind but also historically inevitable. The language used to describe this activity has been sometimes theological and sometimes derived from a secular philosophical worldview.

Of course, the social reality of what happened has been less glorious than the picture offered us by the intellectual justifications. The disjuncture between reality and justifications has been felt acutely, and expressed in multiple ways, by those who paid the biggest price in their personal and collective lives. But the disjuncture has also been noted by various intellectuals whose social origins were in the dominating strata. Hence, the history of the modern world-system has also involved a continuing intellectual debate about the morality of the system itself. One of the first and most interesting of such debates occurred quite early, in the context of the Spanish conquest of much of the Americas in the sixteenth century.

In 1492, Christopher Columbus, after a long and arduous trip across the Atlantic Ocean en route to China, landed on several islands in the Caribbean Sea. He did not find China. But he found something unexpected that today we call the Americas. Other Spaniards soon followed in his path. Within a few decades, Spanish conquistadores had destroyed the political structures of the two largest empires of the Americas—the Aztec and the Inca. Immediately, a motley band of their followers laid claims to land, and sought to use the labor of the populations in these empires and elsewhere in the Americas forcibly and ruthlessly to profit from this appropriated land. Within a half century, a large part of the indigenous population had been destroyed by weapons and disease. How large a part has been a matter of dispute, both in the sixteenth century and the post-1945 years. But most scholars today believe it was an extremely large part.[1]

---

[1] Bartolomé de Las Casas wrote the *Brevíssima relación de la destrucción de las Indias* (1994) in 1552. It was a devastating account that aroused public opinion in Spain at the time. An English translation appears as *The Devastation of the Indies: A Brief Account* ([1552] 1974). The post-1945 discussion of acute population decline is quite extensive. One major work, which launched a good deal of the recent discussion, is that of Sherburne F. Cook and Woodrow Borah (1971).

A canonical figure of the time was Bartolomé de Las Casas. Born in 1484, he came to the Americas in 1502, and was ordained a priest in 1510, the first to be ordained in the Americas. He was initially favorable to and participated in the Spanish system of *encomienda,* which involved the assignment *(repartimiento)* of Amerindians as forced labor to Spaniards managing agricultural, pastoral, or mining properties. But in 1514, he had a spiritual "conversion" and renounced his participation in the encomienda system, returning to Spain to commence his life's work of denouncing the injustices wrought by the system.

Las Casas sought to influence both Spanish and Church policy by participating in many commissions, and writing memos and books. He moved in high circles, being received and even favored at times by Emperor Charles V (King Charles I of Spain). There were some initial successes for the cause he espoused. In 1537, Pope Paul III issued the bull, *Sublimis Deus,* in which he ordained that Amerindians could not be enslaved and could be evangelized only by peaceful means. In 1543, Charles V edicted the *Leyes Nuevas,* which enacted much of what Las Casas had proposed for the Americas, including the end of further concessions of encomiendas. Both the papal bull and the royal decree, however, encountered considerable resistance from the *encomenderos* along with their friends and supporters in Spain and the Church. Eventually, both the papal bull and the *Leyes Nuevas* were suspended.

In 1543, Las Casas was offered the bishopric of Cuzco, which he refused, but he then accepted the lesser bishopric of Chiapas in Guatemala (today located in southern Mexico). As bishop, he insisted on a strict enforcement of the *Leyes Nuevas* by mandating that confessors require of encomenderos the penitence of restitution to the Amerindians, including their liberation from the obligations of encomienda. This interpretation expanded somewhat on Charles V's decree, which was not intended to be applied to those encomiendas that had been previously granted, and in 1546, Las Casas abandoned the bishopric of Chiapas and returned to Spain.

Las Casas was now encountering a systematic attempt by opponents to refute his arguments theologically and intellectually. One key figure in this effort was Juan Ginés de Sepúlveda. Sepúlveda's first book, *Demócrates primero,* written in 1531, was denied the right of publication. But Sepúlveda persisted. And in 1550, Charles V convened a special juridical panel of the Consejo de Indias to meet in Vallodalid, to advise him about the merits of the Sepúlveda–Las Casas controversy. The panel heard the two men successively, but it seems the Junta never gave a definitive verdict. When Charles V was succeeded on the throne a few years later by his son Philip, the Las Casas viewpoint lost all traction with the court.

All that we have today are the documents that the two contestants prepared for this debate. Because these documents posed clearly a central question with which the world is still concerned today—Who has the right to intervene, and when and how?—it is worth reviewing their arguments carefully.

Sepúlveda wrote a second book specifically for this debate: *Demócrates segundo* ([1545?] 1984). It bears the subtitle, *About the Just Causes of the War Against the Indians.* In it, he made four different arguments in defense of the policies of the Spanish government, as interpreted and carried out by the encomenderos. He brought to bear as evidence a long series of references to the established intellectual authorities of the time: in particular, Aristotle, St. Augustine, and St. Thomas Aguinas.

Sepúlveda's first argument was that Amerindians are "barbarians, simple, unlettered, and uneducated, brutes totally incapable of learning anything but mechanical skills, full of vices, cruel and of a kind such that it is advisable they be governed by others." The second contention was that "the Indians must accept the Spanish yoke, even if they don't wish to, as rectification [enmienda, emendentur] and punishment for their crimes against divine and natural law with which they are tarnished, especially idolatry and the impious custom of human sacrifice."

The third reason was that the Spaniards are obliged by divine and natural law to "prevent the harm and the great calamities [the Indians] have inflicted—and which those who have not yet been brought under Spanish rule continue today to inflict—on a great number of innocent people who are sacrificed each year to idols." And the fourth argument was that Spanish rule facilitates Christian evangelization by allowing Catholic priests to preach "without danger, and without being killed by rulers and pagan priests, as has happened three or four times."[2]

---

[2] These quotations are all from the summary by Las Casas ([1552] 2000, 6–8) of Sepúlveda's arguments. The summary is entirely fair, as can be seen by going to Sepúlveda ([1545] 1984). The index compiled by Angel Losada for this edition of Sepúlveda contains the following entry: "War against the Indians—Justifications: (1) natural servitude, 19–39; (2) eradicate idolatry and human sacrifices, 39–61; (3) free innocent people from being sacrificed, 61–63; (4) propagation of the Christian religion, 64" (152). The index is briefer than Las Casas's summary, but it is essentially the same. Reading Sepúlveda's wordy text, especially on the first two arguments, adds little to the summary as a statement of his views.

As one can see, these are the four basic arguments that have been used to justify all subsequent "interventions" by the "civilized" in the modern world into "noncivilized" zones—the barbarity of the others, ending practices that violate universal values, the defense of innocents among the cruel others, and making it possible to spread the universal values. But of course these interventions can only be implemented if someone has the political/military power to do so. This was the case with the Spanish conquest of large parts of the Americas in the sixteenth century. However strong these arguments were as moral incentives for those who did the conquering, it is clear that they were greatly reinforced by the immediate material benefits the conquests brought to the conquerors. Ergo, anyone who was located within the conquering community and wished to refute these contentions was faced with an uphill task. Such a person had to argue simultaneously against both beliefs and interests. This was the task Las Casas set himself.

To the first argument that there are people who are naturally barbarous, Las Casas responded in several ways. One was to note the multiple, and quite loose, ways in which the term barbarous was used. Las Casas said that if someone is defined as barbarous because one engages in savage behavior, then we could find such people in all parts of the world. If one is considered barbarous because one's language is not written, the language could be written, and on doing this, we would discover it to be as rational as any other language. If we restrict the term barbarous behavior to mean truly monstrous behavior, however, then it must be said that this kind of behavior was a quite rare phenomenon, and was in fact constrained socially within all peoples to more or less the same degree.

What Las Casas objected to in Sepúlveda's argument was the generalization to an entire people or political structure of behavior that was that of a minority at most—a minority the likes of which one might as easily find in the self-defined more civilized group as in the group considered to be barbarous. He reminded the reader that the Romans had defined the ancestors of the Spaniards as barbarous. Las Casas was putting forward an argument of the rough moral equivalence of all known social systems, such that there is no natural hierarchy among them that would justify colonial rule (Las Casas [1552] 2000, 15–44).

If the argument about natural barbarism was abstract, the one that the Indians had committed crimes and sins that should be rectified and punished was much more concrete. In this particular case, the claim centered around idolatry and human sacrifice. Here, Las Casas was dealing with questions that aroused quite rapidly the moral repugnance of sixteenth-century Spaniards, who could not understand how anyone could be allowed to be idolatrous or engage in human sacrifice.

The first issue that Las Casas raised was jurisdiction. He pointed out, for example, that Jews and Muslims inhabiting Christian lands might be required to obey the laws of the state, but could not be punished for following their own religious precepts. This was a fortiori true if these Jews or Muslims were living in lands other than those governed by a Christian ruler. Jurisdiction of this kind could only extend, he maintained, to a Christian heretic because a heretic was someone who had violated a solemn pledge to adhere to the doctrines of the Church. If the Church did not have jurisdiction over non-Christians resident in Christian lands, it was therefore all the more unreasonable to argue that the church had jurisdiction over those who had never even heard of its doctrines. Consequently, idolatry might be judged by God, but it was not subject to the jurisdiction of a human group external to the group that practiced it.

Of course, we might today consider Las Casas's argument to be the advocacy of moral relativism, or at least legal relativism. It was subject then, as now, to the attack that this view demonstrated indifference to the suffering of innocents, who were the victims of these practices contrary to natural law. This was Sepúlveda's third, and strongest, contention. And Las Casas treated it prudently. First of all, he insisted that an "obligation to liberate innocents . . . does not exist when there is someone more suitable to liberate them." Second, he said that if the Church had confided the task of freeing the innocents to a Christian sovereign, "others should not take actions in this regard, lest they do it petulantly." But finally, and most important, Las Casas put forward the argument that one must be careful to act in accordance with the principle of minimal damage:

> Although we recognize that the Church has the obligation to prevent the unjust death of innocents, it is essential it be done with moderation, taking care that a greater harm not be done to the other peoples which would be an impediment to their salvation and make unfruitful and unrealized the passion of Christ. ([1552] 2000, 183)

This was a crucial point for Las Casas, and he illustrated it with the morally difficult issue of rituals in which the slaughtered body of children were eaten. He started by noting that this was not a custom among all Indian groups, nor were many children sacrificed among those groups who engaged in the practice.

But this would seem to be an evasion of the issue, were not Las Casas to face up to the reality of a choice. And here, he argued the principle of minimal damage:

> Furthermore, it is incomparably a lesser evil that a few innocents die than that the infidels blaspheme against the adorable name of Christ, and that the Christian religion be defamed and hated by these people and others who learn of this, when they hear that many children, elderly, and women of their race have been killed by the Christians without a reason, as part of what happens in the fury of warfare, as has already occurred. (187)

Las Casas was implacable against what we would today call collateral damage: "it is a sin meriting eternal damnation to harm and kill innocents in order to punish the guilty, for it is contrary to justice" (209).

He came up with a final reason why it was not licit for the Spaniards to punish Indians for the sins the Indians might be committing against innocents. It is "the great hope and presumption that such infidels will be converted and correct their errors . . . [since] they do not commit such sins obstinately, but certainly . . . because of their ignorance of God" (251). And Las Casas ended the discussion with a peroration:

> The Spaniards penetrated, certainly with great audacity, this new part of the world, of which they had never heard in previous centuries, and in which, against the will of their sovereign, they committed monstrous and extraordinary crimes. They killed thousands of men, burned their villages, took their cattle,

destroyed their cities, and committed abominable crimes with no demonstrable or specific excuse, and with monstrous cruelty against these poor people. Can such sanguinary, rapacious, cruel and seditious men be truly said to know God, to whose worship they exhort the Indians? (256)

The answer to this question led straight to the one given by Las Casas to Sepúlveda's last argument: facilitating evangelization. Men can only be brought to Christ through their free will, never by coercion. Las Casas acknowledged that Sepúlveda made the same statement, but Las Casas asked whether the policies that Sepúlveda was justifying were compatible with the concept of free will:

> What greater coercion can there be than that brought by an armed force that opens fire with harquebuses and bombardments, the horrible din of which, even if it has no other effect, makes everyone breathless, however strong they are, especially those who are unacquainted with such weapons and do not know how they work? If the clay pots pop off with the bombardments, and the ground trembles, and the sky is clouded by thick dust, if the old, the young, and the women fall down and the huts are destroyed, and everything seems shaken by the fury of Bellona, would we not truly say that force is being used to get them to accept the faith? (296)

Las Casas believed that war was not a way to prepare souls to suppress idolatry. "The gospel is spread not with lances, but with the word of God, with a Christian life and the action of reason" (300). War "engenders hate, not love, for our religion. . . . The

Indians must be brought to the faith with meekness, charity, a saintly life and the word of God" (360).

If I have spend so much time spelling out the arguments of two sixteenth-century theologians, it is because nothing that has been said since has added anything essential to the debate. In the nineteenth century, the European powers proclaimed that they had a civilizing mission in the colonial world (Fischer-Tiné and Mann 2004). Lord Curzon, Viceroy of India, expressed this ideological perspective well in a speech he gave at the Byculla Club in Bombay on November 16, 1905, to a group composed largely of British colonial administrators:

> [The purpose of the empire] is to fight for the right, to abhor the imperfect, the unjust or the mean, to swerve neither to the right hand nor to the left, to care nothing for flattery or applause or odium or abuse ... but to remember that the Almighty has placed your hand on the greatest of his ploughs ... to drive the blade a little forward in your time, to feel that somewhere among those millions you have left a little justice or happiness or prosperity, a sense of manliness or moral dignity, a spring of patriotism, a dawn of intellectual enlightenment, or a stirring of duty, where it did not before exist. That is enough. That is the Englishman's justification in India. (cited in Mann 2004, 25)

This justification was no doubt somewhat less convincing to the Indian people than it seemed to Lord Curzon and the colonial administrators he was addressing, since Curzon's successors had to quit India less than a half century later in 1948. Perhaps Curzon's Englishmen had not left enough justice, happiness, or prosperity. Or perhaps they had stimulated too much manliness, moral dignity, and patriotism—the latter on behalf of the wrong country. Or perhaps the intellectual enlightenment that the British colonial administrators promoted allowed the likes of Jawaharlal Nehru to draw different conclusions about the merits of British rule. Or perhaps, most devastating of all, the Indian people agreed with Mahatma Gandhi's famous quip in response to a reporter's question: "Mr. Gandhi, what do you think of Western civilization?" "I think," replied Gandhi, "it would be a good idea."

The second half of the twentieth century was a period of massive decolonization throughout the world. The immediate cause and consequence of this decolonization was an important shift in the dynamics of power in the interstate system resulting from the high degree of organization of the national liberation movements. One by one, and in a cascading sequence, the erstwhile colonies became independent states, members of the United Nations, protected by the doctrine of noninterference by sovereign states in the internal affairs of each other—a doctrine enshrined both in evolving international law and the United Nations Charter.

In theory, this should have meant the end of interference. But of course it didn't. To be sure, the justification of Christian evangelization was no longer available to legitimate imperial control, nor was that of the religiously more neutral concept of the civilizing mission of colonial powers. The rhetorical language now shifted to a concept that came to have new meaning and strength in this postcolonial era: human rights. In 1948, the United Nations had erected as its ideological centerpiece the Universal Declaration of Human Rights, which was ratified by almost every member of the United Nations. It did not constitute international law but rather incarnated a series of ideals to which the member nations committed themselves in principle.

Needless to say, there have since been repeated, widespread, and egregious acts that constituted violations of the declaration. Because most governments have grounded their foreign policy in a so-called realist view of interstate relations, almost no intergovernmental action has been undertaken that could be said to reflect this concern with human rights, although the violation of the declaration has been regularly invoked as propaganda used by one government to condemn another.

The virtual nonexistence of intergovernmental concern with human rights questions led to the emergence of many so-called nongovernmental organizations (NGOs) to fill the void. The NGOs that assumed the burdens of direct action to sustain human rights throughout the world were of two main varieties. On the one hand, there was the kind represented by Amnesty International, which specialized in publicizing what it considered illegitimate and abusive imprisonments of individuals. It sought to mobilize the pressure of international public opinion, directly and via other governments, to induce changes in the policies of the accused governments. And on the other hand, there was the kind represented by Doctors Without Frontiers, which sought to introduce direct humanitarian assistance in zones of political conflict, without accepting the mantle of neutrality that had long been the principal strategic shield of the International Red Cross.

This nongovernmental activity had a certain limited degree of success and consequently spread, especially beginning in the 1970s. In addition, this human rights thrust received an impetus by some new activities at the intergovernmental level. In 1975, the United States, the Soviet Union, Canada, and most of the countries of Europe met together at the Conference on Security and Cooperation in Europe (CSCE) and signed the Helsinki Accords, which obliged all the signatory states to observe the Universal Declaration of Human Rights. Since there was no enforcement mechanism for this accord, however, a nongovernmental Western structure, the Helsinki Watch, was created to assume the task of putting pressure on the governments of the Soviet bloc to observe these rights.

When Jimmy Carter became president of the United States in 1977, he asserted that the promotion of human rights would be a centerpiece of his policy, and extended this concept beyond its application in the Soviet bloc (where geopolitically the United States had little purchase) to the authoritarian and repressive regimes in Central America (where geopolitically the United States had considerable purchase). Yet Carter's policy did not last long. Whatever impact it had in Central America, it was essentially revoked during the subsequent presidency of Ronald Reagan.

In this same period, there were three important direct interventions in Africa and Asia, where one government took action against another, using as its argument that the country being attacked was violating humanitarian values. First, in 1976, a Palestinian guerrilla group hijacked an Air France plane with many Israelis aboard and flew it to Uganda, with the complicit accord of the Ugandan government. The hijackers demanded the release of certain Palestinians in Israel in return for releasing the Israeli hostages. On July 14, 1976, Israeli commandos flew into Entebbe airport, killed some Ugandan guards, and rescued the Israelis. Second, on December 25, 1978, Vietnamese troops crossed the Cambodian border, overthrew the Khmer Rouge regime, and installed a different government. And third, in October 1978, Idi Amin of Uganda attacked Tanzania, which counterattacked, its troops eventually reaching the Ugandan capital, overthrowing Idi Amin, and installing a different president.

What is the same in these three instances is that the justification from the intervenors' point of view was human rights—defense against hostage taking in the first case, and undoing extremely vicious and dictatorial regimes in the latter two cases. Of course, in each case, we could discuss the strength and veracity of the charge, and the degree to which no more lawful or peaceful alternative existed. We could also debate the consequences of each of these actions. But the point is that the intervenors argued and believed that they were acting in ways that maximized justice, and therefore were morally justified in natural law, if not legally justified in international law. Furthermore, the intervenors all sought and received considerable approbation not only from their own communities but from elsewhere in the world-system, on the grounds that only the violent means used could have eradicated the patent evil that they asserted was occurring.

What we were seeing was a historical reversion of theorizing about the moral and juridical codes of the world-system. For a very long period, going more or less from the long sixteenth century to the beginning/middle of the twentieth century, the Sepúlveda doctrine—the legitimacy of violence against barbarians and the moral duty to evangelize—predominated, and the Las Casas objections represented a distinctly minority position. Then, with the great anticolonial revolutions in the middle of the twentieth century, and especially in the period 1945–70, the moral right of the oppressed peoples to refuse the paternal oversight of the self-styled civilized people came to have ever greater legitimacy in the world political structures.

Perhaps the high moment of the collective institutionalization of this new principle was the adoption by the United Nations in 1960 of the Declaration on Granting Independence to Colonial Countries and Peoples, a subject that had been totally evaded in the original United Nations Charter written a mere fifteen years earlier. It seemed that Las Casas was at last having his views adopted by the world community. But no sooner was this validation of the Las Casas perspective made official doctrine than the new emphasis on the human rights of individuals and groups became a prominent theme of world politics, and this began to undermine the right to reject paternal oversight. The human rights campaign essentially restored the Sepúlveda emphasis on the duty of the civilized to suppress barbarism.

It is at this moment that the world saw the collapse of the Soviet Union and the dethroning of Communist governments throughout east/central Europe. These events might still be thought to fit within the spirit of the United Nations' declaration on the right to independence. The subsequent breakup of Yugoslavia into its constituent republics, however, led to a series of wars and quasi-wars, in which the struggle for independence became linked to policies of "ethnic purification." The constituent republics of the erstwhile Socialist Federal Republic of Yugoslavia all had long had a clear ethnic focus, but each also had important national minorities. Thus, when they divided up into separate states, a continuing process over a number of years, there was considerable internal political pressure within each of them to reduce or remove entirely ethnonational minorities from the new sovereign states. This led to conflicts/wars within four of the former Yugoslav republics: Croatia, Bosnia, Serbia, and Macedonia. The story of each was rather different, as were the outcomes. But in each, ethnic purification became a central issue.

The continued high level of violence, including rapes and slaughters of civilians, led to calls for Western intervention in order to pacify the region and guarantee a semblance of political fairness, or so it was argued. Such interventions occurred most notably and particularly in Bosnia (with three ethnicities more or less of the same size) and Kosovo (a largely Albanian region of Serbia). When Western governments hesitated, intellectuals and NGOs in these countries stubbornly pressured their states to intervene, and the states eventually did so.

For various reasons, this nongovernmental pressure was strongest in France, where a group of intellectuals founded a journal called *Le Droit d'Ingérence* the [*Right to Intervene*]. While these intellectuals did not cite Sepúlveda, they used secular arguments that pushed in the same direction. They too insisted that "natural law" (although they may not have used this locution) required certain kinds of universal behavior. They too insisted that when such behavior did not occur, or worse still when opposite kinds of behavior prevailed in a certain zone, the defenders of natural law not only had the moral (and of course political) *right* to intervene but the moral and political *duty* to intervene.

At the same time, there were a number of civil wars in Africa—Liberia, Sierra Leone, Sudan, and above all Rwanda, in which there was a mass slaughter of Tutsi by Hutu, without any meaningful intervention by foreign troops. Rwanda, Kosovo, and various other zones of acute human drama became the subject of much retrospective debate about what might or might not have been done, or what ought to have been done, to safeguard human life and human rights in these zones. Finally, I do not need to remind anyone of the degree to which the U.S. invasion of Iraq in 2003 was justified as necessary to rid the world of a dangerous and vicious dictator, Saddam Hussein.

On March 2, 2004, Bernard Kouchner gave the twenty-third annual Morgenthau Memorial Lecture at the Carnegie Council on Ethics and International Affairs. Kouchner is perhaps the world's most prominent spokesperson today for humanitarian intervention. He is the founder of Doctors Without Borders; the coiner of the phrase *"le droit d'ingérence"*; at one time a cabinet minister in the French government charged with human rights concerns; subsequently the Special Representative of the UN secretary-general in Kosovo; and in his own words, someone who has "the added reputation of having been Mr. Bush's only supporter in France." It is therefore of some interest to hear what, on reflection, Kouchner considers to be the place of humanitarian intervention in international law:

> There is an aspect of humanitarian intervention that has proved rather difficult to implement: I refer to the tension between state sovereignty and the right to interfere. The international community is working on a new system of humanitarian protection through the UN Security Council; yet globalization clearly does not herald an end of state sovereignty, which remains the bulwark of a stable world order. To put it another way: we cannot have global governance or a UN system without the sovereignty of states.
>
> The international community must strive, in the pattern of

the European Union, to resolve this inherent contradiction: how can we maintain state sovereignty yet also find a way to make common decisions on common issues and problems? One way to resolve the dilemma is to say that sovereignty of states can be respected only if it emanates from the people inside the state. If the state is a dictatorship, then it is absolutely not worthy of the international community's respect. (2004, 4)

What Kouchner offered us was the twenty-first century's equivalent of evangelization. Whereas for Sepúlveda, the ultimate consideration was whether a country or people were Christian, for Kouchner, the ultimate consideration was whether or not they were democratic (that is, not living in a state that was a "dictatorship"). Sepúlveda could not deal with, and thus totally ignored, the case of countries and peoples that were Christian, but nevertheless engaged in barbaric acts violating natural law, such as Spain and the Inquisition. What Kouchner could not deal with, and thus totally ignored, was the case in which a country or people that has strong popular support might nonetheless engage in barbaric acts against a minority, such as what happened in Rwanda. Actually, of course, Kouchner was in favor of outside intervention in Rwanda, not because it was a dictatorship, but because he considered the acts barbaric. The talk of a dictatorship as a general principle was a fig leaf for this concern, applying in some cases (say, Iraq), but certainly not, in all cases in which Kouchner and others thought it morally imperative to intervene.

Suppose, facing the "inherent contradiction" of which Kouchner spoke—that between the sovereignty of states and common decisions on human rights—we applied the Las Casas principles—his four answers to Sepúlveda—to the situations in Kosovo or Iraq. The first question with which Las Casas dealt was the presumed barbarity of the other against whom one is intervening. The first problem, he said, is that it is never totally clear in these debates who are the barbarians. In Kosovo, was it the Serbs, the government of Yugoslavia, or a particular group of people headed by Slobodan Milošević? In Iraq, was it the Sunni Arabs, the Baath party, or a particular group of people headed by Saddam Hussein? The intervenors moved murkily among all these targets, seldom clarifying or making distinctions, and always arguing the urgency of the intervention. In effect, they were claiming that they would somehow sort out the apportionment of guilt later. But of course later never comes. For a murky opponent allows one to assemble a murky coalition of intervenors, who severally may have different definitions of who are the barbarians, and therefore have different political objectives in the process of the intervention.

Las Casas insisted on sorting all this out in advance. For he argued that true barbarity is a rare phenomenon, normally constrained by the social processes of every social group. If that is so, one of the questions we need always to ask, when faced by a situation among others that we define as barbaric, is not only why did the internal process break down but also the degree to which it did in fact break down. Of course, engaging in such an analytic exercise tends to slow one down, which is the major argument invoked against doing it. There is no time, say the intervenors. At each moment, the situation deteriorates further. And this may well be true. But a slower pace may save one from making grievous mistakes.

The analysis deriving from the Las Casas principle presses us also to engage in a comparison. Are the countries and peoples that are intervening also guilty of engaging in barbaric acts? And if so, are these acts so much less serious than those found among the target countries and peoples such that they justify the sense of moral superiority on which any intervention is based? Certainly, since evil exists everywhere, this kind of comparison could be paralyzing, which is the major assertion against it, and which may also well be true. Yet the attempt at comparison can also serve as a timely brake on hybris.

There is the second Sepúlveda principle: the obligation to punish those who commit crimes against natural law, or as we would say today, crimes against humanity. Some acts may outrage the sense of decency of honest people organized in that nebulous, almost fictive character known as the "international community."[3] And when that happens, are we not obliged to punish such crimes? It is to this argument that Las Casas opposed three questions: Who defined them as crimes, and were they so defined at the time they were committed? Who has jurisdiction to punish? Is there someone else more fit than we to engage in the punishment, if punishment is merited?

The question of the definition of the crimes, and by whom, is of course a central debate, today as in the past. In the Balkan conflicts of the 1990s, there were undoubtedly crimes committed by most people's definitions, including the definitions of the political leaders of the region. We know this because the contending political leaders on all sides accused each other of crimes, and in-

---

[3] See the marvelous, and rather acerbic, commentary on the international community by Trouillot (2004, 230): "I think of [the international community] as a sort of Greek chorus of contemporary politics. No one has ever seen it, but it is singing in the background and everyone is playing to it."

deed the same kind of crimes—ethnic cleansing, rapes, and cruelty. The problem that faced outsiders to the region was which crimes to punish, or rather, how to weigh the relative responsibilities of all the sides.

The intervening outsiders in fact engaged in two kinds of actions. On the one hand, they engaged in first diplomatic and then military action to stop the violence, which in many cases meant siding with one faction or the other in particular situations. This involved at the best a judgment of the relative weight of the crimes, in some sense. On the other hand, the outsider intervenors set up special international judicial tribunals that sought to punish particular individuals, and to select such individuals from all sides of the conflicts.

In the aftermath, in the most spectacular trial following the events, that of Milošević, the heart of Milošević's defense was not merely that he was innocent but that the international criminal tribunal had not indicted various persons from the intervening powers who he charged were guilty of crimes as well. Milošević asserted that the courts were the tribunals of the strong indicting the leaders of the militarily weaker and not courts of justice. So, we had two questions: Were the alleged crimes true crimes or were they merely accepted general behavior? And if they were true crimes, were all the criminals being brought to justice, or only those who were of the country that was the object of the intervention and not those of the country that engaged in the intervention?

The question of jurisdiction was of course central to the debate. On the one side, those who insisted on the right and duty to intervene asserted that establishing the international tribunals was an advance in international law. But juridically, there was the question not only of the procedure by which such a court was established but the narrow geographic definition of its potential jurisdiction.

And finally, there was the issue of whether there were alternative ways of handling the crimes, or alternative handlers. In effect, in the early 1990s, the United States was arguing that the proper handlers were the Europeans—that is, the West Europeans—on the grounds that the Balkans were in Europe and were indeed potential members of the European Union. But the Europeans hesitated, for political and military reasons, to assume this burden without the active support of the United States, and ultimately it was the North Atlantic Treaty Organization (NATO) that assigned itself the task. But it was NATO and not the United Nations primarily because the Western countries feared, probably correctly, that Russia would veto any resolution of the Security Council that singled out an action against Serbia and exempted the other parties to the conflict.

The same questions emerged, with even greater clarity, when it came to the intervention in Iraq by the United States in conjunction with a so-called coalition of the willing. The United States attempted to get Security Council endorsement for its military action. But when it was clear that the United States would get only four out of fifteen votes for an enabling resolution, it withdrew its proposed resolution and decided to move on its own without UN legitimation. The Las Casas question then became even more relevant: By what right did the United States assume jurisdiction in this arena, especially since a large number of the countries of the world openly opposed its actions? The U.S. government's answer was twofold. On the one hand, it argued self-defense on the grounds that the Iraqi government posed an imminent threat to the United States and the world, on the basis of its supposed stock of weapons of mass destruction and its presumed readiness to share these weapons with nonstate "terrorists." This argument subsequently fell to pieces in light of postinvasion knowledge that such weapons were not in the possession of the Iraqi government, and because of widespread disagreement with the contention that Saddam Hussein had such weapons, he would have been willing to distribute them to nonstate "terrorists."

In view of the weakness of this case, the U.S. government fell back on the claim that Saddam Hussein was an evil man who had himself committed crimes against humanity and therefore eliminating him from power was a moral good. And at this point, the question not only of the truth of these assertions but even more of the jurisdiction comes to the fore, as well as whether the moral crimes of Saddam Hussein were the true motive of the outside intervention, given the previous support of the U.S. and other governments for Saddam Hussein at moments in time when he committed precisely the acts that were the basis of the accusation.

Once again, in this situation as in most, the strongest case for the interventions was the defense of the innocent—the innocent Bosnian Muslims who were being raped and slaughtered, the innocent Kosovars who were being evicted from their lands and chased across borders, and the innocent Kurds and Shiites who were being oppressed and killed by Saddam Hussein. What do we learn from the third Las Casas answer to Sepúlveda? Las Casas insisted on the principle of "minimal damage." Even if all the allegations were absolutely correct, would the punishment do more harm than it prevented? The principle of minimal damage is the Las Casas translation to collective social phenomena of the ancient adjunction in the Hippocratic oath to doctors: "Do no harm!"

In the case of the Balkan conflicts, one might perhaps maintain that there has been minimal damage. The active violence was vastly reduced. On the other hand, the ethnic cleansing was not erased or reversed to any great extent; rather, its results were more or less institutionalized. There was no (or only minimal) restitution of property or the right to residence. And the Serbs in Kosovo certainly felt that they were worse off than before. One can raise the question of whether the situation would have ended up in the same place even without the outside intervention. But one cannot make a strong case that the situation was made significantly worse.

One can make that case, however, in regard to the intervention in Iraq. To be sure, Saddam Hussein and the Baath party were no longer in power and could not continue the kinds of oppressive acts in which they had previously engaged. Yet the country suffered from a significant number of negatives that were not true before the outside intervention. The economic well-being of the citizens was probably less. The everyday violence had massively increased. The country became a haven for precisely the kind of militant Islamists against whom the action was presumably directed and who were not really able to operate within the country before the intervention. And the civil situation of Iraqi women became considerably worse. At least one hundred thousand Iraqis were killed and many more severely wounded since the intervention. One might certainly have invoked the principle of minimal damage here.

The final Sepúlveda argument was the right and duty to

evangelize, and the presumed obstacles to that posed by the Amerindians. The equivalent in the twenty-first century is the right and duty to spread democracy. This has been one of the principal contentions of the U.S. and U.K. governments, particularly invoked by U.S. neoconservative intellectuals and Prime Minister Tony Blair. Las Casas insisted that it was meaningless to evangelize by force, that conversion to Christianity had to come from voluntary adherence from within the person converted, and that force was counterindicated.

The same argument was adduced in critiques of the interventions in the Balkans and Iraq insofar as they were justified on the basis that they promoted democracy. It was a question of how one measures conversion to democratic values. For the intervenors, it seemed to mean essentially the willingness to hold elections in which multiple political parties or factions could participate with a minimal degree of civility and the ability to campaign publicly. This was a very minimal definition of democracy. Even at this minimal level, it was far from certain that this had been achieved with any lasting power in either region.

If, however, one meant by democracy something more extensive—genuine decision-making control by the majority of the population in the governmental structure, the real and continuing ability of all kinds of minorities to express themselves politically as well as culturally, and an acceptance of the continuing need and legitimacy of open political debate—it seems quite certain that these are conditions that must mature internally from within different countries and regions, and that outside intervention is in general counterindicated, for it associates the concept with outside control and the negatives brought about by the intervention.

The question—Whose right to intervene?—goes to the heart of the political and moral structure of the modern world-system. Intervention is in practice a right appropriated by the strong. But it is a right difficult to legitimate, and is therefore always subject to political and moral challenge. The intervenors, when challenged, always resort to a moral justification—natural law and Christianity in the sixteenth century, the civilizing mission in the nineteenth century, and human rights and democracy in the late twentieth and twenty-first centuries.

The case against intervention has always come from two sources: the moral doubters among the strong peoples (those invoking the Las Casas arguments), and the political resisters among those against whom the intervention is aimed. The moral case of the intervenors is always sullied by the material interests of the intervenors that are being served by the intervention. On the other hand, the moral doubters always seem to be justifying actions that, in terms of their own values, are nefarious. The case of the political leaders of the people against whom the intervention is aimed is always challenged as reflecting the narrow interests of these leaders and not of the people they are leading.

But all of this ambiguity comes within the framework of accepting the values of the intervenors as universal ones. If one observes that these universal values are the social creation of the dominant strata in a particular world-system, however, one opens up the issue more fundamentally. What we are using as a criterion is not global universalism but European universalism, a set of doctrines and ethical views that derive from a European context, and aspire to be, or are presented as, global universal values—what many of its espousers call natural law. It justifies simultaneously the defense of the human rights of the so-called innocent and the material exploitation engaged in by the strong. It is a morally ambiguous doctrine. It attacks the crimes of some and passes over the crimes of others, even using the criteria of what it asserts to be natural law.

It is not that there may not be global universal values. It is rather that we are far from yet knowing what these values are. Global universal values are not given to us; they are created by us. The human enterprise of creating such values is the great moral enterprise of humanity. But it will have a hope of achievement only when we are able to move beyond the ideological perspective of the strong to a truly common (and thus more nearly global) appreciation of the good. Such a global appreciation requires a different concrete base, though, a structure that is far more egalitarian than any we have constructed up to now.

We may approach such a common base one day—even one day soon. That depends of how the world emerges from the present transition from our existing world-system to a different one, which may or may not be better. Yet until we have weathered this transition and entered into this more egalitarian world, the skeptical constraints on our impulsive moral arrogances that Las Casas preached will probably serve us better than the self-interested moral sureties of the Sepúlvedas of this world. Constructing world legal constraints on crimes against humanity has little virtue if these constraints are not as applicable to the powerful as to those whom they conquer.

The Consejo de Indias that met in Vallodalid did not report its verdict. Hence, Sepúlveda won. It is still not reporting its verdict, and as such, Sepúlveda is still winning in the short run. The Las Casas of this world have been condemned as naive, as facilitators of evil, as inefficacious. But they have nonetheless something to teach us—some humility about our righteousness, some concrete support of the oppressed and persecuted, some continuing search for a global universalism that is truly collective and therefore truly global.

2

Can One Be a Non-Orientalist?
Essentialist Particularism

By the eighteenth century, the issues that Sepúlveda and Las
Casas had debated were no longer a matter of fierce debate.
The European world had settled down into a general acceptance
of the legitimacy of its colonial rule in the Americas and other
parts of the world. Insofar as public debate about colonial regions continued at all, it had become primarily a debate about
the rights to autonomy of the European settlers in these regions,
rather than one about how Europeans should relate to the indigenous populations. Nevertheless, the Europeans in their ex-
pansions, travels, and trade were now coming more and more
into contact with populations—particularly in Asia—who were
located in what in the nineteenth century came to be called zones
of "high civilizations"—a concept that included, among others,
China, India, Persia, and the Ottoman Empire.

These were all zones in which large bureaucratic structures,
of the kind we usually call empires, had been constructed at
some time. These world-empires each possessed a lingua franca
that had a written form and a literature. They were each dominated by a major religion that seemed prevalent throughout the
zone, and they each enjoyed considerable wealth. Since, for the
most part, in the eighteenth century the European powers were

not yet in a position to impose themselves militarily in these zones, they were not sure how to think about them. Their initial stance was often one of curiosity and a limited respect, as though they might possibly have something to learn from them. These zones thus entered the European consciousness as relative peers, possible partners, and potential enemies (enemies metaphysically and militarily). It was in this context that in 1721, the Baron de Montesquieu produced his book *Persian Letters*.

Persian Letters is a fictional set of letters presumably written not by European travelers to Persia but by Persian travelers to Europe, and in particular to Paris. In letter 30, Rica writes home that Parisians are fascinated by the exotic dress he wears. Finding this burdensome, he says he adopted European dress in order to blend into the crowd. "Free of all foreign adornments, I found myself assessed more exactly." But sometimes, he said, someone recognized who he was and told others that he was a Persian. To which the reaction immediately was: "Oh, oh, is he a Persian? What a most extraordinary thing! How can one be a Persian?" (Montesquieu [1721] 1993, 83).

This is a famous question, and one that has bedeviled the European mental world ever since. The most extraordinary thing about Montesquieu's book is that it provides no answer whatsoever to this query. For in the guise of writing about Persian mores, Montesquieu was actually primarily interested in discussing European mores. He expressed his views via fictional Persian commentators as a protective device to allow him to make a social critique of his own world. He was indeed sufficiently cautious that he published the book anonymously, and in Holland, then a center of relative cultural freedom.

Notwithstanding European social ignorance of the world of the so-called Oriental high civilizations, the expansion of the capitalist world-economy proved to be inexorable. The Europe-dominated world-system spread from its Euro-American base to encompass more and more parts of the world in order to incorporate them into its division of labor. Domination, as opposed to mere contact, brooks no sense of cultural parity. The dominant need to feel that they are morally and historically justified in being the dominant group and the main recipient of the economic surplus produced within the system. Curiosity and a vague sense of the possibility of learning something in European contact with the so-called high civilizations thus gave way to the need to explain why these zones should be politically and economically subordinate to Europe, despite the fact that they were deemed to be "high" civilizations.

The core of the explanation that was developed was remarkably simple. Only European "civilization," which had its roots in the Greco-Roman world of Antiquity (and for some in the world of the Old Testament as well), could have produced "modernity"—a catchall term for a pastiche of customs, norms, and practices that flourished in the capitalist world-economy. And since modernity was said to be by definition the incarnation of the true universal values, of universalism, modernity was not merely a moral good but a historical necessity. There must be, there must always have been, something in the non-European high civilizations that was incompatible with the human march toward modernity and true universalism. Unlike European civilization, which was asserted to be inherently progressive, the other high civilizations must have been somehow frozen in their trajectories, incapable therefore of transforming themselves into some version of modernity without the intrusion of outside (that is, European) forces.

This was the thesis put forward by those European scholars,

especially in the nineteenth century, who studied these high civilizations. These scholars were called Orientalists because they were from the Occident, the locus of modernity. The Orientalists were a small and hardy band. It was not easy to be an Orientalist. Since these scholars were studying high civilizations with both a written literature and a different religion (a so-called world religion, but one different from Christianity), an Orientalist needed to learn a language that was difficult for a European, and peruse texts that were themselves dense and culturally remote, if the scholar were to understand in some sense how the people of this strange civilization thought about themselves and the world. We would say today that the Orientalist had to be hermeneutically empathetic. During the nineteenth century and the first half of the twentieth century, there were not many such scholars, and virtually every one was a European or North American.

It was only after 1945 that the arguments and cultural premises of this group of scholars came to be subjected to close criticism. Of course, the reason why this occurred then is obvious. After 1945, the geopolitics of the world-system had changed considerably. The war against Nazism had tarnished the essentialist racism from which the Nazis had drawn such terrible conclusions. And even more important, the non-European world about which the Orientalists had been writing was in full political rebellion against Western control of their countries. Anticolonial revolutions were occurring throughout Asia and Africa, and there were internal politico-cultural transformations were occurring in Latin America.

In 1963, Anouar Abdel-Malek published an article that chronicled the impact of these political changes on the world of scholarship. It was titled "Orientalism in Crisis." He analyzed the two main historic premises of the Orientalists. At the level of the problematic, he argued, Orientalists had constituted an abstract entity, the Orient, as an object of study. And at the thematic level, they had adopted an essentialist conception of this object. Abdel-Malek's attack on both these premises was considered at the time intellectually (and politically) radical, although it seems almost commonplace to us now:

> Thus we arrive at a typology based on a real specificity but detached from history, and thus conceived as intangible and essential. It converts the "object" studied into an other, in relation to whom the studying subject is transcendent; we shall have *homo Sinicus, homo Africanus, homo Arabicus* (and why not *homo Aegypticus?*), while man—"normal" man—is the European man of the historical period dating from Greek Antiquity. We can thus see clearly how, between the eighteenth and twentieth centuries, the hegemonism of the possessing minorities exposed by Marx and Engels, and the anthropocentrism dismantled by Freud, go hand in hand with Euro-centrism in the human and social sciences, particularly those which have a direct relation to the non-European peoples. ([1972] 1981, 77–78)

Abdel-Malek was not widely read in the pan-European world outside a small group of specialists, however. It is the book published fifteen years later by Edward W. Said, *Orientalism* ([1978] 2003), that stimulated a wide cultural debate about Orientalism as a mode of knowledge and interpretation of the reality of the non-Western zones of the modern world.

Said's book was a study of the academic field of Orientalism, especially that part of it that dealt with the Arab-Islamic world.

But it was also, and more important, a study of what Said called the "more general meaning" of Orientalism, "a style of thought based on an ontological and epistemological distinction made between 'the Orient' and (most of the time) 'the Occident' " ([1978] 2003, 2). He saw Orientalism as more than a style of thought, though. It was also, he asserted, "a corporate institution for dealing with the Orient, . . . (an) enormously systematic discipline by which European culture was able to manage—and even produce—the Orient politically, sociologically, militarily, ideologically, scientifically, and imaginatively during the post-Enlightenment period" (3).

And then Said added: "To say simply that Orientalism was a rationalization of colonial rule is to ignore the extent to which colonialism was justified in advance by Orientalism, rather than after the fact" (39). For "Orientalism is fundamentally a political doctrine willed over the Orient because the Orient was weaker than the West" (204).

Furthermore, in his view, Orientalism as a way of thought is self-contained and not open to intellectual challenge:

> The Orientalist surveys the Orient from above, with the aim of getting hold of the whole sprawling panorama before him— culture, religion, mind, history, society. To do this he must see every detail through the device of a set of reductive categories (the Semites, the Muslim mind, the Orient, and so forth). Since these categories are primarily schematic and efficient ones, and since it is more or less assumed that no Oriental can know himself the way an Orientalist can, any vision of the Orient ultimately comes to rely for its coherence on the person, institution, or discourse whose property it is. Any comprehensive vision is fundamentally conservative, and we have noted how in the his-

tory of ideas about the Near Orient in the West these ideas have maintained themselves regardless of any evidence disputing them. (Indeed, we can argue that these ideas produce evidence that proves their validity.) (239)

In the Afterword to his book written fifteen years after the original publication, Said contended that the anger and resistance that greeted his book and other making similar arguments was precisely that "they seem to undermine the naive belief in a certain positivity and unchanging historicity of a culture, a self, a national identity" (332).

What then, for Said? He ended his book by insisting that "the answer to Orientalism is not Occidentalism" (328). And in his reflection on his own book and its reception, he insisted on a distinction between postcolonialism, with which he associated himself, and postmodernism, which he criticized for its emphasis on the disappearance of grand narratives. Quite the contrary for postcolonial artists and scholars, Said argued, for whom:

> The grand narratives remain, even though their implementation and realization are at present in abeyance, deferred, or circumvented. This crucial difference between the urgent historical and political imperatives of post-colonialism and post-modernism's relative detachment make for altogether different approaches and results, although some overlap between them (in the technique of "magical realism," for example) does exist. (349)

Montesquieu had asked the question, How can one be a Persian? but he was not really interested in answering it. Or rather, what he was really interested in elaborating were alternate ways of being a European. This is a perfectly legitimate concern. But it indicated a certain aloofness to the real issue of how we can arrive at an appropriate balance between the universal and the particular. Montesquieu of course was a European, writing within a European context and frame of mind, and did not have too many doubts about the reality of universal values, although he had doubts about how others in Europe presented the set of universal values.

Said was by contrast a quintessential hybrid, on the margins of several identities. He was a highly educated humanist scholar, a specialist in the literature of England, and a product of (and professor in) the Western university system. But he was also by birth and allegiance (both emotional and political) a Palestinian, who was deeply offended by the intellectual and political implications of Orientalism as what he called "a style of thought." He maintained there was no way in which one could be a Persian because the stylized concept, the essentialist particular, was an invention of the arrogant Western observer. Yet he refused to replace Orientalism by Occidentalism, and was dismayed by some of the usages that were made of his analyses by persons who utilized him as a reference.

Said himself made explicit use of Foucault's concept of discourse, and its intimate link to and reflection of power structures. He told us that the essentialist discourse of Orientalism was far from the reality of the regions about which they were writing, especially as this reality was viewed and lived by those who were the subalterns being studied and catalogued by the powerful of the world. In effect, he was telling us that words matter, that concepts and conceptualizations matter, that our knowledge frameworks are a causal factor in the construction of unequal social and political institutions—a causal factor, but not at all *the only* causal factor. He called on us not to reject grand narratives but, quite the opposite, to return to them, for they are today only "held in abeyance, deferred, or circumvented."

When we return to grand narratives, we face two different questions, it seems to me. One is to assess the world, I would say the world-system, in which we are living, and the claims of those in power to be privy to, and implementers of, universal values. The second is to consider whether there are such things as universal values, and if so, when and under what conditions we might come to know them. I should like to take up these two questions successively.

There is a sense in which all known historical systems have claimed to be based on universal values. The most inward-looking, solipsistic system normally purports to be doing things in the only way possible, or the only way acceptable to the gods. "Oh, oh, is he a Persian? What a most extraordinary thing! How can one be a Persian?" That is, people in a given historical system engage in practices and offer explanations that justify these practices because they believe (they are taught to believe) that such practices and explanations are the norm of human behavior. These practices and beliefs tend to be considered self-evident, and are not normally a subject of reflection or doubt. Or at least it is considered heretical or blasphemous to doubt them, or even to reflect on them. The rare people who would question the practices and justifications of the historical social system in which they are living are not merely brave but quite foolhardy, since the group will almost surely turn on them, and most often punish them, as impermissible deviants. So we may start with the paradoxical argument that there is nothing so ethnocentric, so particularist, as the claim of universalism.

Still, the strange thing about the modern world-system—what is uniquely true of it—is that such doubt is theoretically legitimate. I say theoretically because, in practice, the powerful in the modern world-system tend to show the claws of orthodox suppression whenever doubt goes to the point of undermining efficaciously some of the critical premises of the system.

We saw this in the Sepúlveda–Las Casas debate. Las Casas raised doubts about the presumed implementation of universal values as preached by Sepúlveda, and as practiced by the conquistadores and the encomenderos in the Americas. To be sure, Las Casas was careful never to challenge the legitimacy of the acts of the Spanish Crown itself. Indeed, he appealed to the Crown to sustain his reading of the universal values—a reading that would have given large space to the particularist practices of the indigenous populations of the Americas. Yet pursuing the line of argument Las Casas launched would of course sooner or later necessarily have called into question the entire power structure of the emperor. Hence the emperor's hesitations. Hence the indecision of the Junta judges in Vallodalid. Hence the de facto burying of the Las Casas objections.

And when the dominant European masters of the modern world-system encountered the "Persians," they reacted first with amazement—How can one be a Persian?—and then with self-justification, seeing themselves as the sole bearers of the only universal values. This is the story of the Orientalism that is "a style of thought," which first Abdel-Malek and then Said took pains to analyze and to denounce.

But what had changed in the world-system in the late twentieth century such that Said was able to do this, and to find a wide audience for his analyses and denunciations? Abdel-Malek gave us the answer. In calling for a "critical revision" of Orientalism, Abdel-Malek said:

> Any rigorous science that aspires to understanding must subject itself to such revision. Yet it is the resurgence of the nations and peoples of Asia, Africa and Latin America in the last two generations that has produced this belated and still reluctant crisis of conscience. A principled demand has become an unavoidable practical necessity, the result of the (decisive) influence of the political factor—that is, the victories of the various national liberation movements on a world scale.
>
> For the moment, it is Orientalism that has experienced the greatest impact; since 1945 it is not only the "terrain" that has slipped from its hands but also the "men," those who yesterday were still the "object" of study, and who today are its sovereign "subject." ([1972] 1981, 1082, 73)

The critical revision that Abdel-Malek and others were calling for in 1963 had its initial effect on the cloistered academic domain of the professional Orientalists themselves. In 1973, a mere ten years later, the International Congress of Orientalists felt compelled to change its name to the International Congress of Human Sciences in Asia and North Africa. To be sure, this was only after heated debate, and a further ten years later, the group did seek to restore the balance slightly by still another change of name to the International Congress for Asian and North African Studies. But the term Orientalist was not resuscitated.

What Said did was to move outside this cloistered domain.

He acted in the wider domain of general intellectual debate. Said rode on the wave of widespread intellectual upheaval reflected in and fostered by the world revolution of 1968. Thus, he was not speaking primarily to the Orientalists. He was speaking rather to two larger audiences. On the one hand, he was addressing all those who were involved centrally or even peripherally in the multiple social movements emerging out of 1968, and who were by the 1970s turning their attention more closely to questions concerning the structures of knowledge. Said was underlining for them the enormous intellectual, moral, and political dangers of reified binary categories, so deeply embedded in the geoculture of the modern world-system. He was saying to them that we must all shout loudly that there are no essential, unchanging Persians (particulars) who lack an understanding of the only values and practices said to be universal.

But Said was also addressing a second audience: all honest, good persons in the institutions of knowledge and the encompassing social institutions we all inhabit. He was saying to them, beware of false gods, of presumed universalisms that not merely mask power structures and their inequalities but are key promoters of, conservers of, existing immoral polarizations. Said was in fact appealing to another interpretation of the presumed universal values of these honest, good persons. In this sense, he was repeating the long quest of Las Casas. And he died amid the same sense of frustration and incompleteness as Las Casas in this pursuit. To appreciate the nature of the quest—for a true balance (intellectual, moral, and political) between the universal and the particular—we must see with whom Said was quarreling. He was quarreling first of all, and most loudly and passionately, with the powerful of the world and their intellectual acolytes, who were not merely justifying the basic inequalities of the world-system that seemed so patently unjust to Said but were also themselves enjoying the fruits of these inequalities.

He was therefore ready not simply to engage in intellectual battle with them but in direct political contestation as well. Said served as a member of the Palestine National Council, and was active in its deliberations. He was a leading voice within it calling on the Palestine Liberation Organization (PLO) to revise its long-standing claims to the entire former British mandate and acknowledge the right of Israel to exist within the 1967 boundaries alongside an independent Palestinian state. As we know, this was the position that the PLO ultimately adopted with the Oslo Accords in 1993. But when, two years later, Yāsir Arafat signed Oslo 2 with the Israelis, arguing that he was implementing this revised position of the PLO, Said felt that Oslo fell far short of an equal arrangement. Said denounced it as a "Palestinian Versailles." He was not shy about taking other positions that put him at odds with much of the Arab world. For example, he denounced Holocaust revisionism, the Iraqi Baath regime at a time when it was still being supported by Washington, and corruption in various Arab regimes. But all that said, he was an uncompromising supporter of a Palestinian state.

Said had a third quarrel, less vociferous but just as heartfelt. This was his dispute with the postmodernists, who had, he thought, abandoned the quest for intellectual analysis and therefore political transformation. For Said, all three issues were part of the same quest: his attacks on the Orientalist scholars, insistence on a morally consistent and firm political position on Palestine, and unwillingness to abandon grand narratives for what he regarded as nonmaterial and immaterial intellectual games.

Hence, we must place Said's book within the context of its times: first, the worldwide sweep of national liberation movements in the post-1945 years, and second, the world revolution of 1968 which was an expression of the demands of the forgotten peoples of the world for their legitimate place in both the power structures of the world-system and the intellectual analyses of the structures of knowledge.

One can summarize the outcome of fifty years of debate in this way: the transformations of the balance of power in the world-system ended the simple certainties about universalism that prevailed for most of the history of the modern world-system and which entrenched the binary oppositions that were deep in all of our cognitive frameworks, and served as the political and intellectual justification of the dominant ways of thinking. What we have not yet done is achieve any consensus on, indeed any clear picture of, an alternative framework—one that would permit us all to be non-Orientalists. This is the challenge before us in the next fifty years. So we must come to the second question that is posed when we seek to construct our grand narratives: Are there such things as universal values at all, and if so, when and under what conditions might we come to know them? That is to say, how can one be a non-Orientalist?

Let us start at the beginning. How does one think one knows that a value is universal? The answer surely is not by its universal/global practice. In the nineteenth century, some anthropologists tried to assert that there were practices that everyone everywhere observed. The most common example was the incest taboo. It has not, however, been difficult to find, constantly, exceptions at some time and place for any such presumed global social practice. And of course, were practices in fact even ap-proximately the same everywhere, there would never have been a need for proselytism of any kind—religious, secular, or political—since proselytism presumes that there are people to convert—that is, people who do not practice the value the prose-lytizers consider to be universal.

Universal values have normally been asserted to be true on one of two grounds: either they have been "revealed" to us via someone or something—a prophet, prophetic writings, or insti-tutions that claim to be legitimated by the authority of such a prophet or prophetic writings; or they have been "discovered" as being "natural" by the insight of exceptional people or groups of people. We associate revealed truths with religions, and natural law doctrines with moral or political philosophies. The difficulty with both kinds of claims is evident. There exist well-known competing claims to any particular definition of universal values. There are multiple religions and sets of religious authorities, and their universalisms are not always compatible with one another. And there are multiple versions of natural law that are quite reg-ularly at direct odds with each other.

Furthermore, we know that those who defend the set of uni-versal values in which they believe are frequently quite passion-ate about the exclusiveness of the truth that they are proclaiming and quite intolerant of alternative versions of universal values. Even the doctrine of the virtue of the intellectual and political tolerance of a multiplicity of views is itself simply one more uni-versal value that is open to being contested, and indeed is almost always contested by some groups within the historical system in which we are now living.

Of course, we can resolve this uncertainty intellectually by as-serting a doctrine of radical relativism and saying that all value systems, without exception, are subjective creations; and that therefore all of them have equal validity, because none of them is in fact a valid universal. The fact is, however, that absolutely no one is really ready to argue radical relativism consistently. For one thing, it is a self-contradictory claim, since radical relativism, by its own criterion, would be only one possible position, no more valid than any other claimed universalism. For another thing, in practice we all fall back on some limits to what we are willing to accept as legitimate behavior, since otherwise we would be living in a truly anarchic world, one that endangered our survival in an immediate way. Or if there is anyone who is truly willing to argue the position consistently, the rest of us would probably label such persons psychotic and imprison than for our safety. I therefore rule out radical relativism as a plausible position since I do not believe anyone really means it.

But if one doesn't accept that universals that are revealed or arrived at by the insight of wise persons are in fact necessarily universal, and one also does not believe that radical relativism is a plausible position, what can one say about the relation of universals and particulars, about the ways in which one can be a non-Orientalist? For there are many avatars of Orientalism that beset us. Those who are exasperated by Eurocentric universalisms often find it tempting to invert the hierarchy, and they do this in one of two ways.

The first is to make the argument that Europe's presumed achievements, those things that we reify as "modernity," were the common aspirations of multiple civilizations as opposed to things that were specific to Europe's attachment to universalist values—since the eighteenth century, since the sixteenth century, since the thirteenth or tenth centuries, it matters little. One then adds that a momentary edge enabled Europeans to halt this process elsewhere in the world, and it is this that explains the political, economic, and cultural differences of the present. This is a sort of "we could have done it just like you" stance. The "Persians" could have conquered Europe, and it would be they then who would be asking, "Oh, oh, is he a European? What a most extraordinary thing! How can one be a European?"

The second is to invert the hierarchy the other way, by pushing this line of argument one step further. The "Persians" were already doing the things we label as modern or leading to modernity long before the Europeans. By a fluke, the Europeans may have momentarily grabbed the ball, primarily in the nineteenth century and a part of the twentieth. But in the long run of history, it was the "Persians," not the Europeans, who have been the exemplars of universal values. We should thus now rewrite the history of the world to make it clear that Europe was for most of the time a marginal zone and is probably destined to remain that.

These arguments are what Said called "Occidentalism" and what I have called "anti-Eurocentric Eurocentrism" (Wallerstein 1997). It is Occidentalism because it is based on the same binary distinctions against which Said was inveighing. And it is anti-Eurocentric Eurocentrism because it accepts completely the definition of the intellectual framework that Europeans imposed on the modern world instead of reopening entirely the epistemological questions.

It is more useful to start this analyses from a realistic standpoint. There is indeed a modern world-system, and it is truly different from all previous ones. It is a capitalist world-economy, which came into existence in the long sixteenth century in Europe and the Americas. And once it was able to consolidate itself, it followed its inner logic and structural needs to expand geographically. It developed the military and technological competence to do this, and was therefore able to incorporate one part of the world after another, until it came to include the entire globe sometime in the nineteenth century. Furthermore, this world-system operated by quite different principles from previous world-systems, although this is not my subject here (see Wallerstein 1995).

Among the specificities of the capitalist world-economy was the development of an original epistemology, which it then used as a key element in maintaining its capacity to operate. It is this epistemology that I have been discussing, that Montesquieu noticed in *Persian Letters,* and that Said attacked so vigorously in *Orientalism.* It is the modern world-system that reified the binary distinctions, and notably the one between universalism (which it claimed that the dominant elements incarnated) and particularism (which it attributed to all those who were being dominated).

But after 1945, this world-system came under heavy attack from within. It was partially dismantled first by the national liberation movements and then by the world revolution of 1968. It has also suffered from a structural undermining of its ability to continue the endless accumulation of capital that is its raison d'être (see Wallerstein 1998). And this means that we are called on not merely to replace this dying world-system with one that is significantly better but to consider how we can reconstruct our structures of knowledge in ways that permit us to be non-Orientalist.

To be non-Orientalist means to accept the continuing tension between the need to universalize our perceptions, analyses, and statements of values and the need to defend their particularist roots against the incursion of the particularist perceptions, analyses, and statements of values coming from others who claim they are putting forward universals. We are required to universalize our particulars and particularize our universals simultaneously and in a kind of constant dialectical exchange, which allows us to find new syntheses that are then of course instantly called into question. It is not an easy game.

3

How Do We Know the Truth?
Scientific Universalism

There have been two contesting modes of universalism in the modern world. Orientalism is one style—the mode of perceiving essentialist particulars. Its roots are in a certain version of humanism. Its universal quality is not a unique set of values but the permanence of a set of essential particularisms. The alternative mode has been the opposite—scientific universalism, and the assertion of objective rules governing all phenomena at all moments of time. Beginning at least in the second half of the eighteenth century, the humanist mode came under severe attack. Many came to perceive an inherent weakness in the claims of humanist universalism. The dominant humanism of the modern world—Western Christian values (transmuted into Enlightenment values)—was cognitively a self-validating doctrine, and therefore could be taxed with being merely a subjective set of assertions. That which was subjective seemed to have no permanence. As such, its opponents said that it could not be universal. Beginning in the nineteenth century, the other principal modern style of universalism— scientific universalism—consequently gained in relative strength in terms of social acceptance. After 1945, scientific universalism became the unquestionably strongest form of European universalism, virtually uncontested.

Whence came this scientific universalism? The discourse of European universalism has always been about certainty. In the modern world-system, the original theological base of certainty came under severe challenge. And while there always remained many whose view of universals were rooted in the revealed truths of the gods, for many others, especially among the social and intellectual elites, the gods were replaced by other sources of certainty. The discourse of Orientalism was about the certainty of essentialist particulars—how one is a Persian, how one is "modern." But when this discourse was rejected as merely subjective and thus open to question (no longer certain), it could be replaced by the certainties of science, as incarnated in Newtonian premises about linearity, determinism, and time-reversibility. Culturally and politically, this was translated by Enlightenment thinkers into the certainties of progress, especially progress in scientific knowledge and its technological applications.

To understand the importance of this epistemological revolution—first the creation and consolidation of the concept of the so-called two cultures, and then within it the triumph of scientific universalism—one must situate it within the structure of our modern world-system. It is a capitalist world-economy. It has been in existence for some five hundred years and has expanded from its initial locus (parts of Europe plus parts of the Americas) to incorporate by the nineteenth century the entire globe in its orbit, becoming the only historical system on the planet. Like all systems, it has had a life: its period of origin, its longish period of ongoing functioning, and its current terminal structural crisis. During its period of normal functioning, it operated by certain rules or constraints within certain physical boundaries that expanded over time. And these characteristics allow us to call it a system. Like all systems, however, it evolved in observable ways that permit us to label it a historical system. That is to say, its description along its itinerary, while retaining some basic systemic features, was always changing or evolving. We can describe its systemic features in terms of cyclical rhythms (changes that return to an equilibrium, perhaps a moving equilibrium), and its historical evolution in terms of secular trends (changes that move away from the equilibrium, eventually far from the equilibrium).

Because of its secular trends, the system inevitably reaches a point far enough from equilibrium that it can no longer function adequately. The oscillations of the system, which previously returned to the moving equilibrium without too much difficulty, now become wilder and more chaotic. That is the point at which our existing world-system has arrived today. The system has begun to bifurcate, meaning that it can go in one of at least two different directions in order to find a new stability, a new order that will be created out of the chaos, and that will not be merely a transformed old system but an entirely new kind. Which fork in the bifurcation the process will take is inherently unpredictable, however, since it will be the result of an endless number of inputs, which could be called random from a macroviewpoint, but that will involve a series of individual choices seen from a microviewpoint.

Allow me to translate this abstract language into a brief analysis of why this means that the modern world-system is currently in a systemic crisis, that we are living through an era that is chaotic and bifurcating, and therefore, that we are collectively in the midst of a global struggle about the kind of world-system we wish to build as the replacement for the collapsing world-system in which we are living.

The fundamental principle of a capitalist world-economy is the endless accumulation of capital. This is its raison d'être, and all its institutions are guided by the need to pursue this objective, to reward all those who do so and punish all those who do not. To be sure, the system is composed of institutions that further this end—most notably, an axial division of labor between corelike and peripheral production processes, regulated by a network of sovereign states operating within an interstate system. But it also requires a cultural-intellectual scaffolding to make it work smoothly. This scaffolding has three main elements: a paradoxical combination of universalistic norms and racist-sexist practices; a geoculture dominated by centrist liberalism; and the seldom noticed, but quite crucial, structures of knowledge based on an epistemological division between the so-called two cultures.

I cannot spell out in detail here how this network of interlinked institutions have operated.[4] I will simply assert that this system has operated extremely efficiently and successfully in terms of its guiding objective for some four to five hundred years. It has been able to achieve an absolutely extraordinary expansion of technology and wealth, but it has been able to do this only at the cost of an ever increasing polarization of the world-system between an upper 20 percent and a bottom 80 percent—a polarization that has been at one and the same time economic, political, social, and cultural.

[4] For an overview of these institutions, see Wallerstein (2004b). For a historical account of their development, see Wallerstein (1974–89).

What is urgent to note is that the secular trends of this system have caused its processes to approach in recent years asymptotes, which are making it impossible to continue to further the endless accumulation of capital. To appreciate this, one must take note of the basic process by which a productive process in a capitalist system has obtained surplus value/profits that could accumulate as capital. Basically, the profits of any enterprise are the difference between the costs of production and the price that the product can realize on the market. Only relatively monopolized products have been able to realize large profits, since competitive products force sales prices down. But even monopolized products have depended for their profit levels on keeping the costs of production down. This is the constant concern of producers.

In this system, there are three main types of costs of production: personnel, inputs, and taxation. Each is of course a complex package, but it can be shown that on average, all three have risen over time as percentages of the potential sales prices, and that in consequence there is today a global profit squeeze threatening the ability to continue the accumulation of capital at a significant rate. This is therefore undermining the raison d'être of the capitalist system, and has led to the structural crisis in which we find ourselves. Let me rapidly discuss why there exist such secular upward trends in the three costs of production.

The fundamental determinant of the costs of personnel has always been the class struggle, which has been a political struggle both at the workplace and in the arena of state politics. In this struggle, the basic tool of the workers has been syndical organization. The basic tool of the employers has been their ability to locate other workers ready to accept lower recompense. A secondary tool of the workers has been that it is to the advantage of employers to maintain steady production and stay in a location, as long as a strong market exists for their products. A secondary tool of the employers has always been their ability to enlist the state machineries to repress worker demands.

The game has been played in the following way. As long as there was ample market for the product, the employer has preferred to stay in place and avoid disruption, acceding if necessary to worker demands for higher compensation. At the same time, this has furthered the development of worker organizations. But once the market for the product became tighter, the employer has more motivation to reduce urgently the costs of personnel. If repression failed as a tactic, the employer could consider relocating the production process to a zone of lower personnel remuneration.

The employer could find such zones wherever there were large pools of rural workers ready to accept low-paid waged employment because the real income that resulted was higher than such newly employed waged workers had previously obtained in their rural locale. As long as the world was basically a rural one demographically, such zones were always easy to find. The only problem with this solution was that after a period of, say, twenty-five to fifty years, the workers in this new zone began to organize and demand higher remuneration, and the employer was back to the original situation. What happened in practice was that sooner or later the employer repeated the displacement of production to yet another zone. It can be shown that this constant relocation of production processes has worked quite well from the perspective of the producers. Today, however, employers face a new simple dilemma. The constant relocations have led to a deruralization of the world, such that there remain few areas into which to transfer production in this manner. And this inevitably means that the cost of remuneration has been rising on average worldwide.

If we turn to the second basic cost of production, the cost of inputs, we can see that a parallel process has been occurring. The most important way to keep down the cost of inputs has been for producers not to pay their full cost. This may seem an absurd idea, but in practice it has been easy to accomplish by means of what economists discreetly term externalizing the cost. There are three kinds of costs producers have been able to divert onto the shoulders of others. The first is the cost of detoxification of whatever dangerous waste is created in the production process. By simply discarding the waste as opposed to engaging in detoxification, producers have saved considerable expense. The second cost that has traditionally not been regarded as an expense to be borne by the producer is the replacement or regeneration of raw materials. And the third cost not borne by the producer, or at most only partially so, has been that of the infrastructure needed to transport either the inputs to the place of production or the finished product to the place of distribution.

These costs have almost always been deferred, and when finally assumed, were paid by the state, which in effect means they were borne in large part by persons other than the producers who benefited from the inputs. But over time, this has become more difficult to do. Global toxification has risen to the point that there is a serious concern with the collective danger of such toxicity and a social demand for ecological repair. To the extent that this has been done, a demand has followed for the internalization of further costs of detoxification. The global depletion of raw materials has led to the creation of more expensive substitutes. And the ever rising costs of infrastructure has led to demands that users assume their costs, at least in greater part. All three societal responses have had the effect of a significant rise in the cost of inputs.

Finally, taxation has been rising steadily for a simple reason. The world has become increasingly democratized as a result of both popular pressure and the need to appease this popular pressure by meeting some of the material demands of the world's working strata. These popular demands have been basically for three things: educational institutions, health care, and guarantees of lifetime income (old-age pensions, unemployment benefits, income during training, and so on). The threshold amounts of such expenditures have been steadily rising, as has the geographic extent of their implementation. The net result has been an increasing imposition of taxation worldwide on the producers.

To be sure, producers have regularly reacted in the political arena against these increasing costs—seeking to reduce the costs of personnel, resist the internalization of costs of production, and reduce tax levels. This is what the movement of "neoliberalism" has been about in the last twenty-five years—an attempt to reverse these increasing costs. The capitalist strata have had periodic and repeated success in this kind of counteroffensive. Yet the reduction of these costs has always been less than their increase in a previous period, such that the overall curve has been an upward ratchet.

But what has the structural crisis of the world-system to do with the structures of knowledge, the university systems of the world, and scientific universalism? Everything! The structures of knowledge are not divorced from the basic operations of the modern world-system. They are an essential element in the functioning and legitimation of the political, economic, and social structures of the system. The structures of knowledge have historically developed in forms that have been most useful to the maintenance of our existing world-system. Let me review three aspects of the structures of knowledge in the modern world-system: the modern university system, the epistemological divide between the so-called two cultures, and the special role of the social sciences. All three were essentially nineteenth-century constructions. And all three are in turmoil today as a consequence of the structural crisis of the modern world-system.

We regularly talk of the university as an institution developed in western Europe in the Middle Ages. This makes a nice story, and permits us to wear lovely gowns at university ceremonies. But it is really a myth. The medieval European university, a clerical institution of the Catholic Church, essentially disappeared with the onset of the modern world-system. It survived in name only from the sixteenth to the eighteenth centuries since, during this period, it was virtually moribund. It certainly was not the central locus of the production or reproduction of knowledge at that time.

One can date the reemergence and transformation of the university from the middle of the nineteenth century, although there were beginnings of this process from the late eighteenth century on. The key features that distinguish the modern university from that which Europe had in the Middle Ages is that the modern university is a bureaucratic institution, with full-time paid faculty, some kind of centralized decision making about educational matters, and for the most part full-time students. Instead of the curriculum being organized around professors, it is now organized within departmental structures, which offer clear paths to obtaining degrees, which in turn serve as social credentials.

By the end of the nineteenth century, these structures were not only in principle the locus of the reproduction of the entire corpus of secular knowledge but also the principal locus of further research and therefore the production of knowledge. The new kinds of structures then either diffused from western Europe and North America, where they were first developed, to other parts of the world, or were imposed on these other areas as a result of Western dominance of the world-system. By 1945, there were such kinds of institutions virtually everywhere in the world.

It was only after 1945, however, that this worldwide university system reached its full flourishing. There was an enormous expansion of the world-economy in the period 1945–70. This fact, combined with constant pressure from below to increase admissions to university institutions plus growing nationalist sentiment in peripheral zones to "catch up" with leading zones of the world-system, led to an incredible expansion of the world university system—in terms of numbers of institutions, faculty, and students. For the first time, the universities became more than the reserved ground of a small elite; they became truly public institutions.

The social support for the world university system came from three different sources: the elites and the governments, which needed more trained personnel and more fundamental research; the productive enterprises, which needed technological advances that they could exploit; and all those who saw the university system as a mode of upward social mobility. Education was popular, and after 1945 especially, the provision of university education came to be considered an essential social service.

Both the drive to establish modern universities after the middle of the eighteenth century and then the post-1945 push to increase their number opened the question of what kind of education would be offered within these institutions. The first drive—to re-create the university—came in the wake of the new intellectual debate that emerged in the second half of the eighteenth century. As I have noted, the secular humanism of the philosophers had been struggling for at least two centuries, and more or less successfully, against the previous hegemony of theological knowledge. But then it in turn came under severe attack from groups of scholars who started to call themselves scientists. Scientists (the word itself is a nineteenth-century invention) were those who agreed with the humanist philosophers that the world was intrinsically knowable. The scientists, however, insisted that truth could only be known via empirical investigation leading to general laws that explained real phenomena. From the scientists' point of view, the secular humanist philosophers were offering merely speculative knowledge that was not epistemologically different from what had long been offered by theologians. The knowledge offered by the philosophers could not represent truth, they argued, since it was not in any way falsifiable.

Over the nineteenth and twentieth centuries, the scientists put forward one main claim to social support and social prestige. They were able to come up with kinds of knowledge that could be translated into improved technologies—something that was well appreciated by those in power. Thus, scientists had every material and social interest in advocating and achieving the so-called divorce between science and philosophy, a rupture that led to the institutionalization of what would later be termed the two cultures. The most concrete expression of this divorce was the split of the historic medieval faculty of philosophy into two. The resulting names of faculties varied according to the university, but generally, by the mid-nineteenth century, most universities had a faculty reserved to the natural sciences and one reserved to what was usually called the humanities, or the arts, or *Geisteswissenschaften.*

Let me be clear about the nature of the epistemological debate that underlay this separation into two faculties. Scientists maintained that only by using the methods they preferred—empirical research based on and/or leading to verifiable hypotheses—could one arrive at "truth"—a truth that was universal. Practitioners of the humanities contested this assertion strongly. They insisted on the role of analytic insight, hermeneutic, sensibility, or empathetic *Verstehen* as the road to truth. The humanists claimed that their kind of truth was more profound and just as universal as that which underlay the scientists' generalizations, which were often seen as hasty. But even more important, the practitioners of the humanities insisted on the centrality of values, of the good and the beautiful, in the pursuit of knowledge, whereas the scientists asserted that science was value-free, and that values could never be designated as being true or false. Therefore, they said, values lay outside the concern of science.

The debate got more shrill as the decades went by, with many on each side tending to denigrate any possible contribution of those on the other side. It was a question of both prestige (the hierarchy of claims to knowledge) and the allocation of social resources. It was also an issue of deciding who had the right to dominate the socialization of the youth through the control of the educational system, particularly the secondary school system. What one can say about the history of the struggle is that, bit by bit, the scientists won the social battle by getting more and more people, and particularly persons in power, to rank them higher, even much higher, than the practitioners of humanistic knowledge. After 1945, with the centrality of new, complicated, and expensive technology in the operation of the modern world-system, the scientists pulled far ahead of the humanists.

In the process, a de facto truce was established. Scientists were given priority in—and in the eyes of society, exclusive control over—the legitimate assertion of truths. The practitioners of humanistic knowledge for the most part came to cede this ground and accepted being in the ghetto of those who sought, who merely sought, to determine the good and the beautiful. This, more than the epistemological divide, was the real divorce. Never before in the history of the world had there been a sharp division between the search for the true and the search for the good and the beautiful. Now it was inscribed in the structures of knowledge and the world university system.

Within the now separate faculties for each of the two cultures, there then occurred a process of specialization that has come to be called the boundaries of "disciplines." Disciplines are claims to turf—claims that it is useful to bound sectors of knowledge in terms of the object of research and the methods that are used to study these objects. We all know the names of the principal disciplines that were widely accepted: astronomy, physics, chemistry, and biology, among others in the natural sciences; Greek and Latin (or Classics), various national literatures (according to the country), philology, art history, and philosophy, among others in the humanities.

The organization of disciplines brought into being a further separation of knowledge over and above that between the two cultures. Each discipline became a university department. Degrees were awarded for the most part in a specific discipline, and faculty appointments were to a particular department. In addition, transversal organizational structures developed, cutting across universities. Disciplinary journals came into existence, and they published articles primarily or only by persons in those disciplines—articles that concerned (and only concerned) the subject matter that these disciplines purported to cover. And in the course of time, first national, then international, associations of scholars in particular disciplines were created. Finally, and not least important, by the end of the nineteenth century, the so-called great libraries began to create categories that were the mirror image of the disciplinary organization, which all other libraries (and indeed booksellers and publishers) then felt obliged to accept as the categories with which to organize their work.

In this division of the world of knowledge between the natural sciences and the humanities, there was the special and ambiguous situation of the social sciences. The French Revolution had led to a general legitimation of two concepts not widely accepted prior to it: the normality of sociopolitical change, and the sovereignty of the "people." This created an urgent need for governing elites to understand the modalities of such normal change, and fostered a desire to develop policies that could limit or at least channel such change. The search for such modalities and by derivation social policies became the domain of the social sciences, including an updated form of history based on empirical research.

The epistemological question for the social sciences was and has always been where its practitioners would stand in the battle of the two cultures. The simplest answer is to say that social scientists were deeply divided on the epistemological issues. Some of them pushed hard to be part of the scientistic camp, and some insisted on being part of the humanistic camp. What almost none of them did was to try to evolve any third epistemological stance. Not only did individual social scientists take sides in what some called the *Methodenstreit,* but whole disciplines tended to take sides. For the most part, economics, political science, and sociology were in the scientific camp (with individual dissenters, of course). And history, anthropology, and Oriental studies were generally in the humanistic camp. Or at least this was the story up to 1945. After that, the lines became more blurred (Wallerstein et al. 1996).

As the modern world-system began to come into structural crisis, which is something I believe that began to play itself out in and after the world revolution of 1968, all three pillars of the structures of knowledge of the modern world-system started to lose their solidity, creating an institutional crisis parallel to, and part of, the structural crisis of the world-system. The universities began to reorient their social role amid great uncertainty as to where they were heading or ought to be heading. The great division of the two cultures came under severe questioning from within both the natural sciences and the humanities. And the social sciences, which had flourished and was full of self-confidence as never before in the immediate post-1945 years, became scattered and fragmented, and began to utter loud wailings of self-doubt.

The basic problem for the world university system was that it was growing in size and costs exponentially, while its socioeconomic underpinnings were slowing down because of the long stagnation in the world-economy. This led to multiple pressures in different directions. The top intellectuals in the academy became a scarcer phenomenon as a percentage of the total, simply because the numerator was far more stable than the denominator. The result of this was an increase in the bargaining power and therefore the cost of this top stratum, who used their situation to obtain massive reductions in teaching loads as well as huge increases in pay and research funds. At the same time, university administrators, faced with a decline in the faculty/student ratio, were seeking to increase in one way or another teaching loads, and were also creating a two-tier system of faculty, with a privileged segment alongside underpaid, part-time faculty. This has had the consequence of what I call a trend to the "secondary-schoolization" of the university, a long-term downplaying of research along with an increase in teaching responsibilities (particularly large classes).

In addition, because of the financial squeeze, universities have been moving in the direction of becoming actors in the marketplace—by selling their services to enterprises and governments, and by transforming their professors' research results into patents they can exploit (if not directly, then at least by licensing). But to the extent that universities have been moving down these lines, individual professors have been taking their distance from, and even moving out of, university structures—either in order to exploit their research findings themselves or out of distaste for the commercial ambiance of the universities. When this discontent combines with the bargaining power that I have already discussed, the result can be an exodus of some of the top scholars/scientists. To the extent this occurs, we may be returning to the pre-1800 situation in which the university was *not* the primary locus of the production of knowledge.

At the same time, the two-culture divide began to become unhinged. Two major knowledge movements have arisen in the last third of the twentieth century: complexity studies in the natural sciences, and cultural studies in the humanities. While it seems on the surface—to participants in these movements as well as analysts of them—that they are quite different, and indeed antagonistic to each other, there are some important similarities between the two knowledge movements.

First of all, both were movements of protest against the historically dominant position within their field. Complexity studies was basically a rejection of the linear time-reversible determinism that prevailed from Sir Isaac Newton to Albert Einstein, and that had been the normative basis of modern science for four centuries. The proponents of complexity studies insisted that the classical model of science is actually a special case, and indeed a relatively rare one, of the ways in which natural systems operate. They claimed that systems are not linear but rather tend to move over time far from equilibrium. They maintained that it is intrinsically, and not extrinsically, impossible to determine the future trajectories of any projection. For them, science is not about reducing the complex to the simple but explaining ever greater layers of complexity. And they thought that the idea of time-reversible processes is an absurdity, since there exists an "arrow of time" operating in all phenomena, including not only the universe as a whole but every microscopic element within it.

Cultural studies was similarly a rejection of the basic concept that had informed the humanities: that there are universal canons of beauty and natural law norms of the good, and that these can be learned, taught, and legitimated. Although the humanities always claimed to favor the essentialist particular (as against scientific universals), the proponents of cultural studies insisted that the traditional teachings of the humanities incarnated the values of one particular group—Western, White men of dominant ethnic groups—who arrogantly asserted that their particular sets of values were universal. Cultural studies insisted, in contrast, on the social context of all value judgments, and therefore the importance of studying and valuing the contributions of all other groups—groups that had been historically ignored and denigrated. Cultural studies professed the demotic concept that every reader, every viewer, brings a perception to art productions that is not only different but equally valid.

Second, both complexity studies and cultural studies, starting from different points on the spectrum, each concluded that the epistemological distinction of the two cultures is intellectually meaningless and/or detrimental to the pursuit of useful knowledge.

Third, both knowledge movements ultimately placed themselves on the domain of the social sciences, without explicitly saying so. Complexity studies did this by insisting on the arrow of time, the fact that social systems are the most complex of all systems, and that science is an integral part of culture. Cultural studies did this by maintaining that one cannot know anything about cultural production without placing it within its evolving social context, the identities of the producers and those who partake of the production, and the social psychology (mentalities) of everyone involved. Moreover, cultural studies asserted that cultural production is a part of, and deeply affected by, the power structures in which it is located.

As for the social sciences, they found themselves in an ever increasing blurring of the traditional disciplines. Virtually every discipline had created subspecialties that added the adjective of another discipline to its own name (for example, economic anthropology, social history, or historical sociology). Virtually every discipline had begun to use a mix of methodologies, including those once reserved to other disciplines. One could no longer identify archival work, participant observation, or public opinion polling with persons of particular disciplines.

As well, new quasi-disciplines have emerged and even grown strong in the past thirty to fifty years: area studies of multiple regions, women's and gender studies, ethnic studies (one for each group politically strong enough to insist on it), urban studies, development studies, and gay and lesbian studies (along with other forms of studies revolving around sexualities). In many universities, these entities have become departments alongside the traditional ones, and if not departments, they were established as at least so-called programs. Journals and transversal associations have developed parallel to the older disciplinary associations. Besides adding to the swirl of the social sciences by creating ever more overlapping boundaries, they have also made the financial squeeze more acute, as ever more entities competed for essentially the same money.

It seems clear to me, if one looks twenty to fifty years ahead, that three things are possible. It is possible that the modern university may cease to be the principal locus of the production or even reproduction of knowledge, although what would or could replace it is scarcely discussed. It is possible that the new epistemologically centripetal tendencies of the structures of knowledge may lead to a reunified epistemology (different from both of the two principal existing ones) and what I think of, perhaps provincially, as the "social scientization of all knowledge." And it is possible that the social science disciplines will collapse organizationally and be subject to, or perhaps forced into by administrators, a profound reorganization, whose outlines are most unclear.

In short, I believe that the last and most powerful of the European universalisms—scientific universalism—is no longer unquestioned in its authority. The structures of knowledge have entered a period of anarchy and bifurcation, just like the modern world-system as a whole, and whose outcome is similarly anything but determined. I believe the evolution of the structures of knowledge is simply a part of—and an important part of the evolution of the modern world-system. The structural crisis of one is the structural crisis of the other. The battle for the future will be fought on both fronts.

4

The Power of Ideas, the Ideas of Power:
To Give and to Receive?

I have been seeking to show how the realities of power in the modern world-system fashioned over the past five hundred years a series of legitimating ideas, which made it possible for those who have power to maintain it. There were three crucial and large-scale notions, all forms of European universalism. I have discussed them successively: the right of those who believe they hold universal values to intervene against the barbarians; the essentialist particularism of Orientalism; and scientific universalism. These three sets of ideas were in fact closely linked to each other, and the sequence of their appearance as central themes in the modern world, and therefore in this discussion was no accident.

The modern world-system could not have been created and institutionalized without the use of force to expand its boundaries and control large segments of its population. Nonetheless, superior, even overwhelming force has never been enough to establish lasting dominance. The powerful have always needed to gain some degree of legitimacy for the advantages and privileges that came with dominance. The powerful needed to gain this legitimation first of all from their own cadres, who were the essential human transmission belts of their power, and without whom they could not have imposed themselves on the larger group who are the dominated. But they also needed to obtain some degree of legitimation from those who they dominated, and this was far harder than obtaining the consent of the cadres, who after all received some degree of immediate reward for playing the role that was asked of them.

If one looks at the arguments encrusted in the various doctrines that were put forth, they always ended up by seeking to demonstrate the inherent superiority of the powerful. And from this inherent superiority, these doctrines derived not merely the capacity to dominate but the moral justification of their domination. Gaining acceptance for the moral right to dominate has been the key element in achieving the legitimation of power. And in order to do that, it had to be demonstrated that the *long-run* effect of the domination was to the benefit of the dominated, even if the *short-run* effect seemed to be negative.

Of course, this was particularly difficult to contend when the mode of domination was that of brutal power, which was the situation in the sixteenth-century Spanish conquest of the Americas. The right to intervene is a doctrine purporting to justify the use of brutal power. It was first debated seriously, and meaningfully, as we have seen, in the arguments between two Spanish intellectuals of that era: Las Casas and Sepúlveda. They were arguing about a basic issue: What rights did Spanish conquistadores in the Americas have in relation to the indigenous populations? or perhaps the reverse, What rights did indigenous populations have in relation to the Spanish conquistadores?

Sepúlveda derived the right to intervene from the basic barbarity of the Amerindians. As we have seen, Sepúlveda asserted that the practices of the Amerindians were so harmful to themselves and others that they had to be restrained physically from engaging in them (akin to an argument that an individual might be so mentally unbalanced that one would harm oneself or others if not placed in an institution). Sepúlveda further maintained that pressure to convert to Christianity was of the greatest possible benefit to the Amerindians in that their souls would thereby be saved.

Given this kind of contention, Las Casas's response was necessarily at the level of not only anthropology but theology. Las Casas denied such rights to the Spaniards on the grounds that the purported evil was something that occurred everywhere and therefore was not special to the Amerindians. And, he continued, the justification of any intervention depended on a calculus in which one measured the damage it inflicted against the gain it claimed to achieve. He raised doubts about the dangers Amerindian practices posed for themselves or others. Las Casas raised questions about whether interfering with these practices, even if they were negative ones, might in fact cause greater harm than good. And as a priest, he insisted that any pressure to achieve conversions obtained them on false grounds and thus the conversions would be theologically unacceptable. Yet beneath these debates at the elevated level that Sepúlveda sought to conduct them, Las Casas tried to expose the underlying socioeconomic realities of Spanish rule, the sheer human exploitation that was occurring, and hence the simple moral wrongs caused by the conquest as well as the establishment of the plantations and other enterprises by the Spanish conquerors.

This debate was not conducted only in the sixteenth century, it has continued ever since. We are, in the post–September 11 "war on terrorism," continuing to hear the equivalent justifications for aggression and military dominance: that it prevents terrible harm done by others; that the effect of the military efforts will be to bring "democracy" to peoples who do not now have it, and will therefore be to their long-run benefit, even if in the short run they suffer all the consequences of the warfare and the dominance.

Today, as in the sixteenth century, this argument is made in order to convince a reasonably large percentage of the cadres who are the necessary transmission belts of the powerful as well as at least some of those who are actually the direct recipients of the domination. We have no real measures of comparative degrees of legitimation in the sixteenth and twenty-first centuries. But it seems plausible to think that the usefulness of what one might call the Sepúlveda mode of justification has worn rather thin. The reason is simple. We have had five centuries to assess the longer-run effects of the use of brutal force, and the claim that these effects are largely positive has come to seem empirically dubious to more and more people. Consequently, the argument no longer serves very well to legitimate the rule of the powerful and the privileged.

Of course, the Sepúlveda mode was already beginning to wear thin in the eighteenth century. This is one of the reasons why the Orientalist mode began to play a bigger role. For one thing, it was hard to treat large zones that were heirs of bureaucratic world-empires (such as China and India) as though they were filled with mere "savages"—whatever definition one gave to the concept of savages. The fact that the powerful had to resort to Orientalism as a mode of justifying their domination intellectually was itself a sign of recognition by the powerful that they were dealing with groups capable of greater immediate resistance to their power, and who could impress the very cadres of the powerful with their qualities.

Orientalism was a more subtle version of Sepúlveda's assertions since its "case studies" were not so-called primitive peoples but so-called high civilizations that were, however, not that of Western Christianity. Orientalism was a mode of reifying and essentializing the other, especially the sophisticated and potentially powerful other, and thereby seeking to demonstrate the inherent superiority of the Western world.

Orientalism was the form of hypocrisy that vice had now to pay to virtue. For the heart of the Orientalist argument was that even if it were true that Oriental "civilizations" were as culturally rich and sophisticated as Western-Christian civilization, and therefore in some sense its peers, it remained the case that they had a small but crucial defect, the same in each of them. It was asserted that there was something in them that made them incapable of proceeding to "modernity." They have become frozen, suffering a sort of cultural lockjaw, which could be considered a cultural malady.

A new argument for political/economic/military/cultural domination was emerging: the powerful were justified in having their privileged position because it made it possible for them to assist the escape of those who were locked into a sort of cul-de-sac. With the aid of the Western world, Oriental civilizations might break through the limits that their own civilizations had placed on their cultural (and of course technological) possibilities. This Western dominance was consequently no doubt a temporary and transitional phenomenon, but one that was essential to the progress of the world, and in the direct interest of those over whom domination was now being imposed. In order to make this kind of argument, one had to "essentialize" the particular characteristics of those being described in their "civilizational" molds, and that is what one means by Orientalism.

After the decline of the argument in favor of the right to intervene, its avatar, Orientalism, worked for a while—convincing, at least partially, both Western cadres and those being dominated, especially the cadres in those zones being dominated. The latter were initially lured by the model of a "modernization" that was in practice "Westernization," and flattered by the egalitarian pretensions of the doctrine (culturally, anyone could be a Westerner; it was simply a matter of education and will). As the decades went by, however, those who were being "assimilated" and thereby becoming Westerners, even Christians, discovered that their assimilation did not in fact lead, as promised, to equality—political, economic, and above all social equality. Hence, by the twentieth century, the utility of Orientalism as a mode of justification also began to wear thin.

To be sure, Orientalism has not entirely disappeared as an argument. We find it today in the discourse about the "clash of civilizations." But while this discourse has had a certain attractiveness for Western cadres, one would have to look long and hard to find adepts in non-Western zones of the world. Or rather, most of these adepts in non-Western zones of the world today invert the contention, finding Western/Christian civilization, which had evolved into Enlightenment thought, to be the deficient and inferior form of human thought, whose domination should be fought precisely in the name of this inverted Orientalism. This is what one means by fundamentalism—including, it might be added, Christian fundamentalism.

It is in the wake of the decline of the utility of Orientalist arguments that we see the rise of the paeans to scientific universalism, science as truth, as the only meaningful mode of understanding the world. The concept of the two cultures—the fundamental epistemological difference between the search for the true and the search for good values—was the last wrench upward of the legitimating process. One might reject the concept of the primitive, and one might move beyond the reifications of Orientalism. Nevertheless, by establishing an epistemological difference between science and the humanities, the assertion remained that the truth that is universal is the one proposed by the scientists and not the humanists. There was a further subtext: while everyone might be "humanistic" and there might be many humanisms, there could only possibly be a single universal truth. And up to now, those with the capacity to discover it were largely located in the powerful zones of the world-system.

The concept of a science that was outside "culture," that was in a sense more important than culture, became the last domain of justifying the legitimacy of the distribution of power in the modern world. Scientism has been the most subtle mode of ideological justification of the powerful. For it presented universalism as ideologically neutral, as unconcerned with "culture" and indeed the political arena, and deriving its justification primarily from the good it can offer humanity through the applications of the theoretical knowledge scientists have been acquiring.

What the emphasis on scientific universalism did was to establish the theoretical virtue of meritocracy, wherein position was awarded exclusively on the basis of competence, measured by sets of objective criteria. And the persons who then entered into the arena of the competent became autonomous judges of their own value and recruitment. It then followed that, if they were in positions of prestige and power in the world of science, they were morally entitled to be there. And since science produced useful technology, the advance of science was to the benefit of everyone.

A not-so-obvious legerdemain then allowed us to assume that access to all social positions, and not merely those in the narrow domain of science, was achieved somehow via merit and was therefore justified. And if particular zones of the world or strata within the system had fewer rewards than other zones or strata, this was because they had not acquired the objective skills that were available to anyone. Ergo, if one had less privilege and power, it was because one had somehow failed the tests for whatever reason—inherent incompetence, cultural provincialism, or perverse will.

It was by brandishing such arguments that after 1945, with the centrality of new, complicated, and expensive technology in the operation of the modern world-system, the scientists pulled far ahead of the humanists. This was all the easier given the severe doubts that now emerged about the essentialist particularisms of the Orientalists. Only science could resolve what were seen as the increasingly immediate problems caused by the polarization of the world-system.

The search for the good was now excluded from the realm of superior knowledge, which meant that there was no ground on which to criticize the logic of these inferences, since one was thereby being anti-intellectual. The structural social constraints that prevented people from entering the higher realms of the meritocracy were basically eliminated from the analysis or allowed to enter it only on the terms of accepting the assumptions of the two cultures in the investigation.

How universal has our universalism been? Once we divided the world into two cultures, universalism became the domain of the scientists, who insisted on a certain methodology, a certain political stance (value-free science), and a corporate insulation from direct social evaluation of their work. It also resulted inevitably in a geographic concentration of the work and the workers that met these criteria, and therefore a degree of unadmitted but real social bias in the work. But most of all, it shielded the powerful from a moral critique by devaluing the plausibility and objectivity of moral critiques. Humanists could be ignored, especially if they were critical humanists, on the ground that they were not scientific in their analyses. It was the final nail in the self-justificatory process of the modern world-system.

The issue before us today is how we may move beyond European universalism—this last perverse justification of the existing world order—to something much more difficult to achieve: a universal universalism, which refuses essentialist characterizations of social reality, historicizes both the universal and the particular, reunifies the so-called scientific and humanistic into a single epistemology, and permits us to look with a highly clinical and quite skeptical eye at all justifications for "intervention" by the powerful against the weak.

A half century ago, Léopold-Sédar Senghor called on the world to come to the *rendez-vous du donner et du recevoir,* the meeting place of giving and receiving. Senghor was perhaps the perfect hybrid of the modern era. He was both a poet and a politician. On the one hand, he was a great exponent of negritude and the general secretary of the Society of African Culture. At the same time, however, he was a member of the Académie française, whose formal task it is to defend and advance French culture. Senghor was the first president of Senegal, but he had previously been a minister in the French government. He was the appropriate person to make this call.

But in today's world, can there be a meeting place of giving and receiving? Can there be a universalism that is not a European but a universal (or global) universalism? Or rather, what would it take, in the twenty-first century, to arrive at a world where it was no longer the West that was giving and the rest that were receiving, one in which the West could wrap itself in the cloak of science and the rest were relegated to peoples who had more "artistic/emotional" temperaments? How can we possibly arrive at a world in which all would give and all would receive?

The intellectual operates necessarily at three levels: as an analyst, in search of truth; as a moral person, in search of the good and the beautiful; and as a political person, seeking to unify the true with the good and the beautiful. The structures of knowledge that have prevailed for two centuries now have become unnatural, precisely because they edicted that the intellectual could not easily move between these three levels. Intellectuals were encouraged to restrict themselves to intellectual analysis. And if they were unable to hold back from expressing moral and political compulsions, the intellectuals were told to segregate the three kinds of activities rigidly.

Such segregation or separation was extremely difficult, probably impossible, to achieve. And it is no accident therefore that most serious intellectuals have always failed to achieve the segregation fully, even if and when they preached its validity. Max Weber is a good case in point. His two famous essays "Politics as a Vocation" and "Science as a Vocation" reveal the nearly schizophrenic ways in which he wrestled with these constraints, and ratiocinated his political involvement to make it look like it was not contradicting his commitment to a value-free sociology.

Two things have changed in the last thirty years. As I have tried to show, the hold that the concept of two cultures has had on the structures of knowledge has weakened considerably, and with it the intellectual underpinning of this pressure to segregate the pursuit of the true, the good, and the beautiful. But as I have also argued, the reason for the massive questioning of the concept of the two cultures is precisely linked to the developing structural crisis of the modern world-system. As we have moved into this era of transition, the importance of fundamental choice has become more acute even as the meaningfulness of individual contributions to that collective choice has grown immeasurably. In short, to the extent that intellectuals shed the constraints of a false value neutrality, they can in fact play a role that is worth playing in the transition within which we all find ourselves.

I want to make myself quite clear. In saying that value neutrality is both a mirage and a deception, I am not arguing that there is no difference between the analytic, moral, and political tasks. There is indeed a difference, and it is fundamental. The three cannot simply be merged. But they also cannot be separated. And our problem is how to navigate this seeming paradox, of three tasks that can neither be merged nor separated. I would remark in passing that this effort is one more instance of the only kind of epistemology that holds hope for the reunification of all knowledge—a theory of the unexcluded middle (Wallerstein 2004a, 71–82).

Of course, this dilemma exists for everyone, not just the intellectual. Is there something special, then, about the role of the intellectual? Yes, there is. What one means by intellectuals are persons who devote their energies and time to an analytic under-standing of reality, and presumably have had some special train-ing in how best to do this. This is no small requirement. And not everyone has wished to become a specialist in this more general knowledge, as opposed to the concrete particular knowledge we all need to perform any task competently. Intellectuals are thus generalists, even if the scope of their expertise is in fact limited to a particular domain of the vast world of all knowledge.

The key question today is how we can apply our individual general knowledge to an understanding of the age of transition in which we live. Even an astronomer or a critic of poetry is called on to do this, but a fortiori this is a demand that is made of social scientists, who claim to be specialists about the mode of functioning and development of the social world. And by and large, the social scientists have been doing it badly, which is why they are on the whole held in such low esteem not only by those in power but also by those opposed to those in power, as well as by the vast numbers of working strata who feel they have learned little of any moral or political use from what social scien-tists have produced.

To remedy this, the first need is the historicization of our in-tellectual analysis. This does not mean the accumulation of chronological detail, however useful that might be. And this does not mean the sort of crude relativization that asserts the ob-vious fact that every particular situation is different from every other, and that all structures are constantly evolving from day to day, from nanosecond to nanosecond. To historicize is quite the opposite. It is to place the reality we are immediately studying within the larger context: the historical structure within which it fits and operates. We can never understand the detail if we do not

understand the pertinent whole, since we can never otherwise
appreciate exactly what is changing how it is changing, and why
it is changing. Historicizing is not the opposite of systematizing.
One cannot systematize without seizing the historical parameters of the whole, of the unit of analysis. And therefore one cannot historicize in a void, as though everything were not part of
some large systemic whole. All systems are historic, and all of
history is systematic.

It is this sense of the need to historicize that has led me here to
place so much emphasis on the argument that not only do we
find ourselves within a particular unit of analysis, the modern
world-system, but within a particular moment of that historical
system, its structural crisis or age of transition. This, I hope (but
who can be certain?), clarifies the present, and suggests the constraints on our options for the future. And this is of course what
most interests not only those in power but also those opposed to
those in power as well as the vast numbers of working strata who
are living their lives as best they can.

If intellectuals pursue the tasks they are called on to pursue in
an age of transition, they will not be popular. Those in power
will be dismayed at what they are doing, feeling that analysis un-
dermines power, especially in an age of transition. Those opposed to those in power will feel that intellectual analysis is all
well and good, provided it feeds and encourages those involved
in political opposition. But they will not appreciate hesitancies,
too much nuance, and cautions. And they shall try to constrain
the intellectuals, even those who claim to be pursuing the same
political objectives as those who oppose those in power. Finally,
the vast numbers of working strata will insist that the intellectuals' analyses be translated into a language they can understand

and with which they can connect. This is a reasonable demand, but not one always easy to fulfill.

Still, the role of the intellectual is crucial. A transition is always a difficult process. There are many shoals against which the process can run aground. Clarity of analysis is often blurred by the chaotic realities and their immediate emotional tugs. But if the intellectuals do not hold the flag of analysis high, it is not likely that others will. And if an analytic understanding of the real historical choices is not at the forefront of our reasoning, our moral choices will be defective, and above all our political strength will be undermined.

We are at the end of a long era, which can go by many names. One appropriate name could be the era of European universalism. We are moving into the era after that. One possible alternative is a multiplicity of universalisms that would resemble a network of universal universalisms. It would be the world of Senghor's *rendez-vous du donner et du recevoir.* There is no guarantee that we shall arrive there. This is the struggle of the coming twenty to fifty years. The only serious alternative is a new hierarchical, inegalitarian world that will claim to be based on universal values, but in which racism and sexism will continue to dominate our practices, quite possibly more viciously than in our existing world-system. So we must all simply persist in trying to analyze a world-system in its age of transition, in clarifying the alternatives available and thereby the moral choices we have to make, and finally, in illuminating the possible political paths we wish to choose.

BIBLIOGRAPHY

Abdel-Malek, Anouar. [1972] 1981. *Civilisations and Social Theory.* Vol. 1 of *Social Dialectics.* Albany: State University of New York Press.

Cook, Sherburne F., and Woodrow Borah. 1971. *Essays in Population History: Mexico and the Caribbean.* Vol. 1, Berkeley: University of California Press.

Fischer-Tiné, Harald, and Michael Mann, eds. 2004. *Colonialism as Civilizing Mission: Cultural Ideology in British India.* London: Wimbledon.

————. [1545?] 1997. *Obras Completas,* III por A. Truyol y Serra: *Demócrates segundo.* Ed. A. Coroleu Lletget. *Apología en favor del libro sobre las causas justas de la guerra.* Trans. Angel Losada. Salamanca: Europa Artes Gráfica.

Hanke, Lewis. 1974. *All Mankind Is One: A Study of the Disputation Between Bartolomé de Las Casas and Juan Ginés de Sepúlveda in 1550 on the Intellectual and Religious Capacity of the American Indians.* De Kalb: Northern Illinois University Press.

Kouchner, Bernard. 2004. Twenty-third annual Morgenthau Memorial Lecture, Harmonie Club, New York, March 2. http://www .carnegiecouncil.org/view/Media.php/prmTemplateID/8/prmID/4 425#2 read on 10/28/2004.

Las Casas, Bartolomé de. [1552] 1974. *The Devastation of the Indies: A Brief Account.* Trans. Herman Briffault. Baltimore, MD: Johns Hopkins University Press.

————. [1552] 1992. *In Defense of the Indians.* Ed. Stafford Poole. De Kalb: Northern Illinois University Press.

————. [1552] 1994. *Brevíssima relación de la destrucción de las Indias.* Ed. José María Reyes Cano. Barcelona: Ed. Planeta.

————. [1552] 2000. *Apología, o Declaración y defensa universal de los derechos del hombre y de los pueblos.* Ed. Vidal Abril Castelló et al.,

Vallodalid: Junta de Castilla y León Consejería de Educación y Cultura.

Mann, Michael. 2004. " 'Torchbearers upon the Path of Progress': Britain's Ideology of a "Moral and Material Progress" in India: An Introductory Essay." In *Colonialism as Civilizing Mission: Cultural Ideology in British India,* ed. Harold Fischer-Tiné and Michael Mann, 1–26. London: Wimbledon.

Montesquieu, Baron de. [1721] 1993. *Persian Letters.* London: Penguin Books.

Prigogine, Ilya. 1997. *The End of Certainty: Time, Chaos, and the New Laws of Nature.* New York: Free Press.

Said, Edward W. [1978] 2003. *Orientalism.* 25th Anniversary edition with a new Preface by the Author New York: Vintage.

Sepúlveda, Juan. Ginés de. [1545?] 1984. *Demócrates segundo, o De las justas causas de la guerra contra los indios.* Ed. Angel Losada. 2nd ed. Madrid: Consejo Superior de Investigaciones Científicas, Instituto Francisco de Victoria.

Trouillot, Michel-Rolph. 2004. The North Atlantic Universals. In *The Modern World-System in the Longue Duree,* ed. Immanuel Wallerstein, 229–237. Boulder, CO: Paradigm Press.

Wallerstein, Immanuel. 1974–89. *The Modern World-System.* 3 vols. New York & San Diego: Academic Press.

———. 1995. *Historical Capitalism, with Capitalist Civilization.* London: Verso.

———. 1997. Eurocentrism and Its Avatars. *New Left Review* 226 (November–December): 93–107.

———. 1998. *Utopistics, or Historical Choices for the Twenty-first Century.* New York: The New Press.

———. 2004a. *The Uncertainties of Knowledge.* Philadelphia: Temple University Press.

———. 2004b. *World-Systems Analysis: An Introduction.* Durham, NC: Duke University Press.

Wallerstein, Immanuel, et al. 1996. *Report of the Gulbenkian Commission on the Restructuring of the Social Sciences.* Stanford, CA: Stanford University Press.

Printed in the USA
CPSIA information can be obtained
at www.ICGtesting.com
LVHW091517080824
787695LV00001B/166